D0939589

Black River Road

Also by DEBRA KOMAR

The Bastard of Fort Stikine
The Lynching of Peter Wheeler
The Ballad of Jacob Peck

BLACK RIVER ROAD

An Unthinkable Crime, an Unlikely Suspect,
and the Question of Character

DEBRA KOMAR

Copyright © 2016 by Debra Komar.

All rights reserved. No part of this work may be reproduced or used in any form or by any means, electronic or mechanical, including photocopying, recording, or any retrieval system, without the prior written permission of the publisher or a licence from the Canadian Copyright Licensing Agency (Access Copyright). To contact Access Copyright, visit www.accesscopyright.ca or call 1-800-893-5777.

Edited by Sarah Brohman.
Cover and page design by Julie Scriver.
Cover image detailed from a work by Randall Roberts, www.etsy.com/market/rrobertsphoto.
Printed in Canada.
10 9 8 7 6 5 4 3 2 1

Library and Archives Canada Cataloguing in Publication

Komar, Debra, 1965-, author
Black River Road : an unthinkable crime, an unlikely suspect, and the question of character / Debra Komar.

Includes bibliographical references and index.
Issued in print and electronic formats.
ISBN 978-0-86492-876-4 (paperback).--ISBN 978-0-86492-848-1 (epub).--ISBN 978-0-86492-804-7 (mobi)

1. Munroe, John A., -1870. 2. Munroe, John A., -1870--Trials, litigation, etc. 3. Vail, Sarah Margaret, 1845-1868. 4. Vail, Ella May, 1868-1868. 5. Murderers--New Brunswick--Saint John. 6. Murder--New Brunswick--Saint John. 7. Trials (Murder)--New Brunswick--Saint John. I. Title.

HV6535.C32N44 2016   364.152'309715   C2016-902279-X
C2016-902280-3

We acknowledge the generous support of the Government of Canada, the Canada Council for the Arts, and the Government of New Brunswick.

Goose Lane Editions
500 Beaverbrook Court, Suite 330
Fredericton, New Brunswick
CANADA E3B 5X4
www.gooselane.com

RECYCLED
Paper made from
recycled material
FSC® C103567

To AC,
and other dodged bullets

The first time someone shows you who they are, believe them.

— Maya Angelou

CONTENTS

The Dahmer Effect

In 1992 a cannibalistic serial killer forced forensic science to redefine what a murderer really is, forever changing the court's understanding of who is capable of committing the act. The new paradigm might surprise you, for the case did not raise the standard — it lowered it to include everyone.

At the trial of Jeffrey Dahmer, the second most controversial man in the courtroom was prominent forensic psychiatrist Park Dietz. It was a tough curve to be graded on, as Dahmer had killed at least seventeen men, often mutilating the bodies before and after death for sexual purposes.[1] These were not the only reasons people thought Dahmer was insane, but they were certainly among them. At a preliminary hearing, Dahmer pled not guilty by reason of insanity. Prosecutors hired Dr. Dietz to challenge that notion. In the months leading up to the trial, Dietz interviewed Dahmer for eighteen hours, much of it spent watching gay porn and violent films. The two men bonded; the doctor later said he found Dahmer's honesty refreshing, even a little endearing.

During the two-week trial Dietz insisted the accused was sane, a declaration that initially drew outrage from the press and the forensic community.[2] A well-circulated joke at that year's annual meeting of the American Academy of Forensic Sciences was, "How many people do you have to eat for Park Dietz to say you're crazy?" Dr. Dietz's assessment did find a receptive audience in the courthouse, however. Jurors rejected Dahmer's insanity defence, declaring him guilty on fifteen counts of murder. He was sentenced to nearly a thousand years in jail but survived only two before a fellow inmate beat him to death.

Dietz's diagnosis of sanity was in keeping with his theory of "universal lethality in people"—the belief that everyone, given the right circumstances, can and will kill.[3] "I think people are born with the inherent ability to be cruel and harmful and destructive and selfish and acquisitive," Dietz told one reporter, adding, "It's the function of many of the institutions of society to train us out of that."[4] According to Dietz, individuals like Dahmer were not insane; they simply had not been conditioned properly. If murder was truly an inherent taboo, the doctor argued, we would not need laws to prevent it.

Dietz's universal lethality theory inverted the widely held (and religiously fostered) notion that human beings are naturally good and that murder is committed by a deviant few suffering from serious defects of character. The theory holds that murder is simply a decision made like any other: a weighing of the risks and rewards of such action. How killers balance that equation may differ from societal norms, but that does not make them evil or insane. The theory simplifies the question of the accused's capacity to kill: if you are capable of making a decision (i.e., legally sane), you are capable of murder.

All higher crimes, including murder, consist of two elements: the mental element (intent, or what the perpetrator is accused of thinking) and the physical element (the prohibited act, or what the defendant is accused of doing). Once the issue of sanity is resolved, every murder trial breaks down to two basic questions: did the accused make the decision to kill, and did he or she act on that decision?

Modern advances in forensic science, such as the advent of DNA, have made tremendous strides in addressing the physical element but contribute nothing to our understanding of the mental component of the crime. Forensic psychiatrists and psychologists may classify the accused's personality disorders or deviations, but they cannot profess to know with any degree of scientific certainty what the perpetrator was thinking in the moments leading up to the murder. The result is a justice system that is out of balance. The law demands evidence of both elements, yet the science presented in court weighs heavily in favour of the physical component. The result is a judiciary forced to cobble together a patchwork of the accused's *perceived* character, personality, and motivations to address the mental element and secure a conviction.

Such efforts are futile, if for no other reason than most people are poor judges of character. What we excel at as a species is projecting our own biases onto others. Although such limitations can prove troublesome in our day-to-day lives, our truncated powers of discernment are crippling when questions of character move from the court of public opinion into an actual courtroom. Religious doctrine implores the faithful to "judge not, lest ye be judged," but the courthouse makes no such demands. A trial is an exercise in scrutiny in which everyone adjudicates the accused's actions and character.

And therein lies the problem. Unlike the scientific testing of physical evidence, there are no objective standards for assessing character. Accordingly, how such evidence is presented to the court has not changed throughout the history of jurisprudence. To illustrate these points, consider the case of John A. Munroe. Munroe was a wealthy, educated man, a respected architect in Saint John, New Brunswick. In 1869 he was accused of a very serious crime. The case holds distinction in Canada's legal pantheon because Munroe was arguably the first to actively defend himself and his character. How his lawyer did it then is exactly how we do it now: the defence had his friends and family take the stand to praise him, while the prosecution called his critics to disparage him.

The question of character was central in Munroe's trial, for the Crown had few other weapons in its arsenal. Forensic science was in its infancy, and physical evidence played little role in any criminal proceeding. The introduction of forensic psychiatry was still decades away. Furthermore, Victorian doctors did not separate the accused's character from his mental health. Clinicians had yet to coin the terms *psychopath* or *sociopath*, and as Wittgenstein later noted, "All I know is what I have words for."[5] The defendant's character, on the other hand, was there for all to see and discuss, and discuss it they did.

Today, such debates are informed by universal lethality theory, which renders the question of character moot in murder trials. By its legal definition, murder must be an intentional act—a decision—or it is not murder (the act becomes a lesser charge, such as manslaughter). The theory separates the issue of character from the decision-making process, creating a philosophical conundrum that is the central thesis of this book: does your character govern your decisions, or do your decisions define your character?

Despite this theoretical de-emphasis on character, the issue continues to infiltrate criminal proceedings in surreptitious ways. The accused's character remains a key issue in homicide trials—not because of the mental element but because the public demands it. We want to know who the defendant is and why he or she committed the crime. The chasm grows ever wider between what the public wants and what the judicial system built to serve that public requires.

Dietz's universal lethality theory has not found widespread public acceptance in part because it is an untestable hypothesis. Forensic psychiatry is a science of opinion rather than empirical evidence. The rules governing the admissibility of evidence for all other forensic sciences—that methods must be "widely accepted" within their respective discipline, and be replicable, reliable, and verifiable[6]—do not (and often cannot) apply to forensic psychiatry. The only way to test the theory would be to strike the laws prohibiting murder from the books and wait to see what happens.

Is everyone capable of murder? The Canadian court certainly believes so, to such an extent it will not allow a defendant to argue the contrary. The law guarantees that everyone is innocent until proven guilty, but the question of capacity is no longer open for debate. In the wake of universal lethality theory, the question has been answered at a population (or indeed species) level, rather than on a case-by-case basis at the level of the individual.

It is not my intention to convince you universal lethality theory is real or that all humans can and will kill; you likely already have strong opinions on the subject. Whether you think the theory is a pessimistic view of humanity, or a realistic one, is entirely up to you. All I ask is that you consider John Munroe's case the way the court requires—that murder is simply a decision everyone is capable of making, and character is irrelevant—rather than through the lens of popular culture. Set aside the questions raised by "murder as entertainment"—whodunit and why—and focus instead on the questions the law dictates: did Munroe make the decision to kill, and did he act on it?

Aberrant, Abhorrent Vapours

George Cunningham was born on the Black River in a village too small to contain his ambitions. A strapping young man full of mirth and brio, Cunningham bid farewell to life on the farm and made his way to the neighbouring city of Saint John, New Brunswick. He immediately joined the ranks of the city's nascent police force and walked a beat for the next four years.[1] There he learned about life and death, although he didn't know death as well as he thought.

Cunningham occasionally returned to the Black River to visit old acquaintances. On April 18, 1869, George rattled over familiar ground in a carriage with his good friends the McNaughtons and two of his sisters, talking of this and that. As the carriage passed Bunker's Tavern and rolled along Black River Road, an indescribable stench assaulted the party, pushing the women to the brink of unconsciousness.[2] The odour was so powerful that Cunningham "could hardly get the horses by it."[3] He whipped the team forward with all his might. When the noxious cloud dissipated, the party regained its composure and the journey continued without further unpleasantness. Cunningham pushed the incident from his mind. For whatever reason, the scent of malfeasance failed to trigger the investigative instincts of one of Saint John's finest.

Later that week, George Parker—a resident of Ten Mile Creek in the parish of Simonds—found himself on the same stretch of road. Parker normally took the Hibernian Road, but on that day he was accompanying another young man on a matter of some urgency. "The day was very fine,"

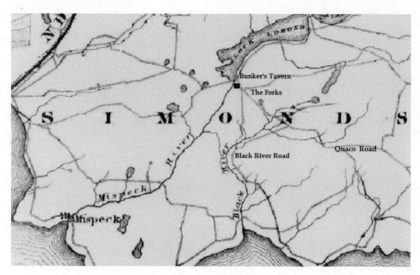

FIG. 1 Detail of the Parish of Simonds, Saint John and
Kings County Plan, New Brunswick, ca. 1870

Parker later said, so the two men were making good time when their
carriage crashed headlong into a wall of fetid rankness. "I never
smelled...anything like that smell before," Parker claimed. "It was a very
bad smell."[4] Parker ploughed through the foulness, gratefully gulping fresh
air on the other side before continuing on his way.

In May, Robert Holmes encountered the fumes after he passed the
fingerboards[5] at The Forks, near the McClellan farm on the river. Holmes
knew the region well because he owned land in the Caledonia Settlement
along Quaco Road. While he could not remember the exact date, he
claimed he would remember the smell until his dying day.[6] His neighbour
Joe Kennedy recalled hitting the stench as late as August.[7] Strangely
enough, none of the locals who lived on the river ever detected the reek
of decay. Perhaps constant exposure had rendered them immune, like
beasts of burden grown impervious to the elements.

Curiosity never got the better of the coach drivers along the road, and
no one accosted by the stench ever went in search of its source. Had any
of them stopped to investigate, this story would have played out very
differently.

ACT ONE

In which a decision is made, or
circumstances conspire against an innocent man.

FIG. 2 The architect John A. Munroe

ONE

Saint John

John A. Munroe was an extremely confident man, but you can only listen to a cock crow so many times before you want to wring its neck. It was a lesson Munroe learned early and well, allowing others — most notably his father — to trumpet his superiority for him.

Munroe also knew how to make an entrance. Born in 1839 in the city of Saint John, his birth predated his parents' marriage by several months, a scandalous turn in so regimented an age. His father, John Jones Munroe, finally made an honest woman of Mary Eleanor Bustin in a ceremony sanctioned by the Reverend J.W.D. Gray on May 22, 1840, while baby John sat in cherubic ignominy on the knee of his paternal grandmother Elizabeth.[1] Five other children — sons George and Frank and daughters Ellie, Lizzie, and Alice — followed in their own time. Four other sons — William, Henry B., Edward, and Charles — did not survive infancy.[2] In defiance of the times, Mary gave birth to her last child when she was forty-three years old,[3] an age beyond the norm in terms of fertility or even life expectancy.

As the love child, John Jr. was indulged from his first breath. He often followed his father to the No. 2 Mechanics Fire Company on Sydney Street, where the elder Munroe served as engineer.[4] John Sr. rose steadily through the ranks of Saint John's burgeoning fire department, becoming assistant chief in 1849. The newly constructed Sydney Street fire station was designed by the city's premier architect John Cunningham. Whether such proximity to genius set young John on his eventual career path cannot be known. What is clear is that, once out of diapers, Munroe's favoured son lost all interest in the shiny red pumper trucks and began to bury his nose in books.

Few traces remain of John's formative years or educational history. He was raised Methodist, his father being one of the founding members of the Centenary Church.[5] He attended a "Sabbath School,"[6] but there is no record of his matriculating from (or even attending) any institution of higher learning. How Munroe qualified as an architect is also misty, although typically young men apprenticed at the feet of seasoned veterans. John likely learned his craft from the aforementioned John Cunningham or perhaps Matthew Stead, who counted the design of the provincial lunatic asylum among his greatest works.[7]

The city and all its architectural wonders were enough for young John Munroe. He never travelled or studied abroad, never spending a single day outside his father's earnest reach.[8] Whatever educational advantages were heaped on John's golden head did not trickle down to his younger siblings. Neither George nor Frank accomplished much of note, though in fairness neither found themselves on the wrong side of the law, either. The Munroe girls all married well enough, which was all that was asked of them. Ellie, the eldest, wed James Gibson, a lawyer from Boundary Creek. Lizzie married Robert S. Craig, an interior decorator in Saint John, while Alice, the youngest, snagged a Wilmot and moved to Seattle.[9]

In 1865 John Munroe Sr. had something of a mid-life crisis. He quit the firehouse to begin crafting wooden valises for the upscale market. He had always been good with his hands, and his venture soon flourished.[10] By that time, his eldest son was well on his way to becoming a draftsman of note, although to hear his father tell it, his son's brilliance already eclipsed the likes of John Cunningham and his venerable ilk.[11]

Whatever his father's embellishments, John A. Munroe was a gifted architect, even if few of his designs still stand today. Many of his more notable creations — including the Wiggins Male Orphans Asylum and the Germain Street Baptist Church[12] — were destroyed in the Great Fire of 1877 that razed much of Saint John to the ground.[13]

Furthermore, his craft agreed with him. He was drawn to the precision and control of architecture. There were those in his profession with greater passion or creativity, but Munroe watched many careers evaporate in a haze of alcohol and regret. Whatever vices Munroe may have possessed, the excesses of drink or virtuosity were not among them.

One of his lesser angels, however, was his vanity.[14] John Munroe's well-oiled facial hair and immaculate wardrobe were a manifestation of his need for grandeur and acclaim or, more to the point, to be seen as grand and acclaimed. For Munroe, the belief that the clothes make the man was held as gospel.[15]

The quest for physical perfection extended to his choice of bride. At the height of the 1862 social season, Munroe married Annie A. Potts in a ceremony befitting their rank.[16] Family fortunes guaranteed the newlyweds a comfortable existence. In May 1865, the couple moved into 45 Charlotte Street in the tony neighbourhood bordering what is now King's Square. The Munroes shared the duplex with William Belding and his wife. The Beldings encountered Munroe "almost every day," and the neighbours thought "nothing wrong of the man as to his character." Indeed, William Belding later claimed he "wouldn't want to live with a better" soul than "the well-behaved" and "gentlemanly" Munroe.[17]

The Charlotte Street address granted the Munroes access to the upper echelon of Saint John society. Munroe's wife and two sons — aged seven and three as our drama begins — were often seen promenading about the square, taking in the air of the city's gentrified core. The architect's punishing work schedule prohibited him from accompanying his family, yet he never failed to provide for their needs.

To meet his own needs, however, John A. Munroe looked far beyond the King's Square.

TWO

Low-Hanging Fruit

Like many unions of the era, John Munroe's marriage to Annie Potts was one of convenience, serving to cement the social status of its participants. She was an appropriate bride, as attractive and well bred as a racehorse, but Annie fell short in one crucial regard: though placid and obedient, she did not *adore* John. Thanks to his father's constant coddling, Munroe came to expect exaltation from those in his immediate circle.[1] Annie was his wife and the mother of his children, but she was not the idolizing mirror Munroe craved.

Sarah Margaret ("Maggie") Vail was everything Annie Potts Munroe was not. From her head to her hems, Maggie was nothing to write home about. She was certainly not the Victorian stereotypical fragile and consumptive female. In an age that favoured its women pleasantly plump, Maggie was well past zaftig. The kindest adjectives her supporters could marshal were "stocky" and "stout,"[2] although one acquaintance went so far as to call her "a lowish sized woman."[3] On a more winsome creature, her skin might be described as alabaster, but on Maggie it was fish-belly white. However, even Maggie's harshest detractors agreed that her hair was her finest feature. She kept it coiffed in the latest styles, an amber mane cascading down her back.[4] Many praised her dazzling smile, although her intimates were quick to note she was snaggle-toothed — one of her upper incisors was longer and wider than its mate, causing her two front teeth to overlap.[5]

Despite Maggie's physical shortcomings, she was universally described as an attractive woman, for there was something beguiling in her spirit. Maggie carried herself well. She kept abreast of the latest fashions, devouring ladies' periodicals and aping the trends to the extent her budget allowed.[6] She also possessed a very pretty face, normally a consolatory compliment to women of size, but in Maggie's case it proved true. In short, Sarah Margaret Vail did the best she could with what she had, and the net result was passable, if not entirely memorable.

Maggie Vail may not have been airbrushed by genetics but John Munroe already possessed such a vision in Annie. What the forgettable and oft-forgotten Maggie offered had nothing to do with pedigree: she grew to adore John with blind, reckless abandon.[7] She knew no better; in matters of the heart, Maggie was a true tabula rasa.

By the time Maggie met Munroe, she was already whiffy with the scent of rejection. She was born on January 26, 1845, the youngest of ten children: four boys and six girls, although one of each soon passed to the heavens. Her mother died when Maggie was just six years old.[8] By the 1860s, she was the only Vail girl left unmarried, a fact her sisters played on with soul-crushing frequency.[9] Maggie was not the poorest excuse among the Vail siblings—that distinction went to William, "the foolish one"[10] confined in the South Bay Provincial Lunatic Asylum—but her desperation made her the sticking place of her family's sharpest barbs. She eventually learned to guard the unbruised part of herself. To her credit she never withdrew nor did she sour; she merely endured. With no viable romantic prospects on her horizon, Maggie remained in the family home in the parish of Lancaster, serving as caretaker to her widowed and ailing father, John.

In the summer of 1865, Maggie took a rare afternoon away from tending hearth and home to venture with her sister Phileanor "Philly" Jane Crear to Mr. McCarthy's Pic-Nic Grounds in Carleton. At five o'clock, the sisters called it a day. They were walking home when two men fell in step behind them. One of the men was John Munroe; the identity of his companion is unknown. The foursome exchanged polite greetings, and Maggie was instantly smitten with the dashing young architect from

Saint John. Munroe, however, was too busy smiling at Phileanor to take much notice of Maggie. There was no question which Vail sister he preferred.[11]

In a naked bid for attention, Maggie picked up a stone, daring her sister to hit a nearby tree. She knew Philly was a poor hand at sports and hoped to embarrass her in front of the men. Munroe saw his opening, telling Philly, "I bet you a quarter you can't strike the tree."[12] Never one to shrink from a challenge, Phileanor threw the rock with all her might, only to watch it sail wide of its mark. The quartet enjoyed some good-natured ribbing at Philly's expense and soon found themselves walking in tandem along the road. At some point Munroe's unnamed partner departed the group, leaving him to escort the ladies home.

The trio eventually arrived at the house of Ephraim Eaton, where Phileanor shared a small apartment with her husband, Robert G. Crear. Maggie brazenly invited Munroe into her sister's home, but the architect declined, claiming he needed to catch the next ferry. Maggie's longing overpowered social convention; she pressed Munroe to stay. Munroe, who still only had eyes for Philly, finally acquiesced, and the three made their way into the parlour. Although she found Munroe's attentions flattering and her sister's pellucid efforts at flirting amusing, Phileanor now feared where all this was heading.

The situation became mortifying when John Munroe finally revealed his interest in Phileanor. He'd assumed both women were unmarried and keeping house together. Indeed, he was so convinced that Philly went to her bureau drawer to retrieve her marriage certificate, which she presented to her crestfallen suitor. Munroe spied the name of the groom, declaring: "I know you now — you are married to Crear in town."[13] Realizing the men were acquainted, Phileanor went in search of her husband, leaving Munroe in her sister's anxious company.

What transpired between Munroe and Maggie during Philly's brief absence was never shared with another living soul. When Philly returned, it was clear Munroe's romantic interest had transferred to the youngest Vail girl. The couple leapt to their feet as Phileanor came back into the parlour while Maggie nervously exclaimed, "I must go home."[14] Munroe stated he, too, would take his leave. The pair then hastily left the room. Philly watched from her window as they made their way down Rowley's Hill toward town.

That evening Phileanor grilled her husband about Munroe. She was outraged to learn he was a married man with children. Scandalized by his forward behaviour, Mrs. Crear prayed she'd seen the last of the wandering-eyed architect, although she suspected Maggie was beseeching the heavens for an entirely different outcome.

The sisters did not speak again for almost a week. Thoughts of Munroe faded from Phileanor's mind, but he was never far from Maggie's. Ten days after their initial meeting, Maggie and John sauntered arm-in-arm toward the Crears' front door, intent on paying their first social call as a courting couple.[15] Maggie beamed as she presented her prized escort to her sister, who stood dumbstruck. Still, Philly felt duty bound to offer them some hospitality. She threw together a modest meal, on which Munroe heaped treacly praise. After the tea service was cleared, the trio sat in awkward silence broken only by a stilted exchange about the weather. Maggie was too ecstatic to notice.[16]

Philly held her tongue for the five hours that passed like a glacier through her parlour, her torment ending only when the couple bid her farewell. Munroe and Maggie left together as darkness fell. Phileanor tried to reach her sister throughout the coming week, but Maggie was deeply infatuated and would not entertain her protestations. The sisters finally agreed to meet at the Crear house the following Sunday. Philly was visibly relieved to see Maggie arrive alone, but her joy evaporated when John Munroe appeared at her door minutes later. Robert Crear was enjoying a rare day's leisure, and the parlour clock's tick filled the void as the men exchanged a few forced pleasantries about the city and their shared business acquaintances. Only Maggie seemed to be having a pleasant afternoon, hanging on Munroe's every utterance.

As six bells sounded the dinner hour, Philly could no longer endure the stagnant tableau. She confronted Munroe, telling everyone he was a married man. Munroe, who had recently celebrated his third wedding anniversary, calmly dismissed the claim. When she repeated her allegation, Munroe insisted he was unmarried. He then asked if she might be mistaking him for his brother George. Phileanor turned to her husband for support, only to find his gaze fixated on the sitting-room rug. Philly insisted Munroe was married to Mr. Potts's daughter Annie, and they had at least one child. The accusation hung in the air as Maggie begged Munroe to say it was not true. Unfazed, he patted Maggie on the hand then turned to Phileanor and laughed. Philly defiantly stood her ground while Munroe refused to yield.

Robert Crear finally intervened, calling his wife into the kitchen, leaving Maggie and Munroe to sort things out. "They were alone together themselves for a long time, and I did not hear what conversation passed between them," Philly later recalled.[17] Sometime after seven o'clock, the Crears returned to the parlour, where it seemed the matter was resolved. A few minutes later, Maggie and Munroe took their leave.

Munroe's secret was finally out — he came equipped with a wife and progeny — but it did not quell Maggie's ardour for her lone gentleman caller. She found herself in a love triangle with some very sharp edges, yet her obsession obliterated any concerns she may have felt. Her life began to revolve around Munroe. "Sometimes he came three or four times a week," Phileanor said, "and if she was not there he used to send for her."[18] She watched as Munroe "used to come backwards and forwards to the house and he and my sister used to meet each other out walking."[19] The couple flaunted their budding romance throughout Carleton and beyond.

Despite their public assignations, Munroe's romantic designs on Maggie were modest. He never displayed any overt signs of affection, and Philly noticed "he did not seem to care much" what Maggie did "as long as it answered his purpose."[20] Munroe offered little of substance, but to Maggie's love-starved heart a trace of something was better than a lifetime of nothing.

In fairness to Maggie, some of Munroe's actions were difficult to decipher. For instance, he was fond of giving gifts. Jewellery was a frequent offering, including a ring he gave Maggie in the spring of 1867.[21] The ring's design bore no resemblance to the promise bands normally exchanged between intimates, yet Maggie wore it as if it were a wedding ring. For his part, Munroe said only that the ring had cost him four dollars, a sum large enough to avoid accusations of thrift but falling well short of a serious commitment. He also gave Maggie a small locket that she wore every day for the rest of her life.

John Munroe bestowed two other remembrances on Maggie Vail during the initial weeks of their courtship, gifts that offer some insight into the nature of their relationship. The first was a tiny silver-plated pistol and a supply of ammunition, a curious memento to cement a romance.[22] The second was a tintype of Munroe, handsomely bound in an ornate frame.[23] He never requested a photo of Maggie in return, but she had a dozen taken and gave him four. Munroe did ask for a photo of the far more lissom Phileanor, a request Philly happily granted.[24] Maggie was stung. In a fit of jealous pique, she commissioned an ambrotype of herself. She mounted the image in an elegant silver locket that she attached to Munroe's watch fob. She had effectively marked her territory, but her gift did not dangle from his timepiece for long.

Phileanor had mixed feelings regarding the adulterous union. She welcomed Munroe into her home and gave him her photo, suggesting some measure of acceptance, yet she continued to berate him for his promiscuous ways. When pressed, he claimed he was powerless to change the situation, saying "he did not know what to do as [Maggie] liked him," and was always "sticking up" for him.[25] The sentiment confused Philly even further.

Jacob Vail, the girls' uncle, offered Maggie some "good advice, telling her [Munroe] was a married man and that she was very foolish in thinking about him at all." His avuncular counsel fell on deaf ears, as he later recalled: "She gave me a good deal of abuse, and I gave her up, and that was the last conversation I had with her."[26] Maggie also fell out with her sister Rebecca Ann Olive "on account of her behaviour with Mr. John Munroe."[27] Maggie remained steadfast, telling her family she loved John Munroe, she was certain he loved her, and the rest did not matter.

In hindsight, Philly Crear could not pinpoint which of the architect's countless visits became "the occasion on which he accomplished [Maggie's] ruin."[28] All Philly knew for certain was that in June 1867, Maggie found herself "in the family way."[29]

THREE

Hollow Threats and Loaded Questions

Maggie hid her delicate condition until she was well into her seventh month. Her stockiness worked to her advantage; no one noticed as she grew thick around the middle. But in the week before Christmas 1867, Phileanor came to stay with Maggie at the family home.[1] Living in such close quarters, Philly soon discovered her sister's ripening secret.

There had been clues all along: John Munroe's visits had dropped off precipitously, and Maggie nagged him incessantly during his rare appearances. "She began to jaw him when he came in for how he had seduced her," recalled Philly.[2] Late one afternoon, following an absence of more than a fortnight, Munroe once again darkened Maggie's door. He stayed only a few minutes. Maggie spent the visit in tears, moaning that "she had no friends left her." Munroe asked, "Ain't I a friend to you?" Maggie petulantly replied he was not, ordering him to "go home to his wife and child."[3]

Their relationship continued to deteriorate as Maggie's due date neared. Munroe arrived at the Vail home unannounced one Saturday evening. He found Phileanor scrubbing the kitchen floor while Maggie rested by the stove. Neither sister rose to greet him. Munroe lifted Maggie from her chair, seated himself in her place then pulled her onto his lap. As the chair groaned under their collective weight, Philly quipped he "must want a load." Munroe fired back that "he could hold four or five the same way,"[4] although the retort did more to defend his own mettle than protect his paramour's wounded honour. Maggie bore the insult in silence.

In earshot of Philly, Munroe then posed a strange question: "Maggie, if I get some poison, will you go and poison my wife?" The query elicited no response from Maggie. Philly simply assumed the architect was talking out of the side of his mouth. She tried to lighten the mood with laughter and another barbed quip: "John Munroe, the day may come when I may have to hold this against you." Munroe left soon after without a word from Maggie.[5]

On February 4, 1868, Dr. M.H. Peters was hastily summoned to the Vail home in Carleton. Peters was a long-time friend of John Vail. He'd served as his personal physician for decades, standing vigil in December 1867 as Vail lay dying. Peters readily diagnosed Maggie's condition as she scurried about her father's sick room, trying desperately to hide her growing belly. When the call came in February, the doctor knew Maggie—unwed and now fatherless—was going to need an inordinate amount of help. There was only so much Peters was prepared to do.

The doctor arrived to find Maggie in the final throes of childbirth. He went to work as the uncomplicated delivery produced a beautiful baby girl. The physician cut the cord, handing the newborn to her flustered Aunt Philly, and turned to attend to the mother.[6]

The birth of an illegitimate child was not normally cause for celebration, but Maggie was delighted. With mother and child resting comfortably, the doctor focused on the necessary paperwork. He was preparing the registration of live birth when he realized he needed the father's name. Given her scandalous circumstances, the question should have been a source of considerable discomfort, but Maggie proudly announced the father was the noted architect Mr. John A. Munroe. The doctor completed a birth certificate in the name Ella May Munroe, keeping his comments to himself.

Phileanor was washing the infant when she noticed something odd. The baby had an unsightly purple bulge on her tiny white abdomen. Peters diagnosed it as an umbilical hernia. He prescribed the remedy of the day, ordering Philly to cut a nutmeg in two and "sew half of it into a little pocket and bind it against the stomach."[7] Peters then headed home.

Ella's hernia worsened despite the folk palliative. Phileanor wrestled with the homemade truss, but "that did not do it any good."[8] Louisa Ells, a lay nurse who lived next door, recommended replacing the nutmeg with a piece of lead. Maggie suggested using one of the bullets from their father's gun. Philly unloaded the weapon, took the bullet to the stone hearth, and beat it flat with an axe. She then used an awl to punch holes in the soft lead disc. Taking up a needle and thread, she stitched it onto a piece of cotton and tied it tight around Ella's tummy, creating an unsightly but effective truss.

Three weeks after the birth, John Munroe paid a call on his misbegotten family. He and Phileanor called a fragile truce. She took him to the nursery and presented the baby to its father, asking, "John, how do you like your child?" Munroe replied, "It is a pretty little thing; it looks like its mother." He never held the child, staying only a few minutes more.[9]

While Maggie lay convalescing, it fell to Phileanor to approach the architect regarding the sticky issue of child support. Munroe initially pled poverty, but Philly was relentless. To silence her Munroe eventually sent a boy with a note containing three dollars. More pressure resulted in a post office dispatch with five dollars, accompanied by explicit instructions to leave him in peace.[10] Philly would not, and Munroe grew frustrated. He had his legitimate children to think of, and it was becoming difficult to maintain two households.

There were other men in Maggie's life willing to play the role of husband, for a price. Chief among them was her brother-in-law James Olive, a shipwright who spent his days in the docklands of Saint John. The sea was his life but didn't provide much of a living, so Olive sought out supplemental sources of income. He often made ends meet by working as a handyman for the local spinsters and widows.[11] The money wasn't much, but he liked feeling needed. Olive lived in Carleton, a few doors down from the Vail house. With no husband for Maggie to call her own, James took to stopping by her house as the need arose, tools at the ready.

When he died, Maggie's beloved father left her the family home, along with a very modest inheritance.[12] She learned to stretch every cent until it snapped, but the money did not last long. Ten months later, John Vail's estate completed probate. Despite her cautious spending, Maggie found herself with nothing left but the house in Lancaster Parish. Her only choices were to continue living in the house and go bankrupt or to sell the property and sustain herself and Ella with the proceeds. Siblings and friends counselled Maggie to keep the family homestead, but she was unsure. Though she had not heard from John Munroe in eight months, she still considered him her most trusted adviser. Her quandary gave Maggie a reason to contact him.

Talk of money always piqued Munroe's interest, and he considered her problem carefully. He advised her to sell, suggesting her future would be greatly improved if she were free of the burden of homeownership. That was all Maggie needed to hear, although what she heard was an implicit offer of a renewed relationship with Munroe.[13] Over the protestations of her closest associates, Maggie put the house on the market and accepted the first offer. John C. Littlehale, a neighbour and friend to John Vail, wanted the property for his son. He offered Maggie five hundred dollars for the house and land.[14] It was a pittance for so desirable a property, but the prospect of a future with John Munroe made money irrelevant in Maggie's eyes.

On October 5, 1868, Littlehale arrived with cash and deed in hand. Maggie could neither read nor write, so she called on James Olive for help. While Maggie rocked a fussy Ella in her arms, James Olive counted out the cash, a mixture of Commercial Bank and St. Stephen's bills.[15] Olive then affixed his signature to the deed as a witness, handing the money to Maggie, who set Ella on the floor. Olive watched as "she took the money and put it in her bosom. She then got a needle and thread and sewed it up."[16]

Maggie grabbed Ella and asked Littlehale if he would take her and her travelling trunk in his carriage to Mr. James Brittain's boarding house, which she planned to call home for the immediate future. The trip was miles out of his way, but Littlehale was a gentleman of the old school, and he reluctantly agreed.[17] James Olive said his goodbyes and returned home. He never saw Maggie or Ella again.

FOUR

Ship of Fools

While Maggie and Ella set down roots in Brittain's boarding house, Munroe made his way back home. He returned to a full social schedule with his wife, Annie, and renewed his enthusiasm for his career. He was determined to put his brief dalliance behind him, recommitting to a life anchored in King's Square. Yet the more he withdrew from her, the tighter Maggie clung. She hoarded anything associated with John Munroe. On the rare occasions he sent child support, he always included a hastily scrawled note asking Maggie not to bother him again. Despite the frosty tone of the missives, she lovingly bundled the notes and placed them in a pretty blue box, cherishing them as if they were sonnets.[1] Maggie gathered the crumbs of affection John occasionally tossed her way, transforming them into a sumptuous banquet. She believed having his child would spur him to make a greater commitment to her. She wanted more; he wanted out. They soon reached an impasse neither party could circumvent without some collateral damage.

In the fall of 1868, the architect planned a tour of Boston "with some gentlemen from the city, partly on business and partly on pleasure."[2] The reason for the trip was to recover some items from a house owned by one of Munroe's travelling companions, Mr. Fenety.[3] There were no plans for Munroe's lawful wife and children to accompany him on the journey. Maggie and Ella were also not included in the itinerary.

The day before he set sail, he stopped by the boarding house to inform Maggie of his plans. She insisted on going with him, but Munroe laughed, assuring her it was not an option. When she asked why, he told her the excursion was strictly business.[4] Thinking the matter closed, Munroe bade her farewell, leaving Maggie in tears.

As the steamer pulled away the following morning, Munroe stood on the deck enjoying the receding view of Saint John. He felt a tap on his shoulder and turned to discover Maggie standing defiantly at the railing. The ensuing squabble lasted until the boat entered Boston Harbor. To broker a truce, Maggie suggested he need "only to keep an eye to her and her trunks while on board," insisting she would make her own way after they docked in Boston.[5]

Once on dry land, Maggie broke her promise by asking Munroe to secure her a coach and take her to a fine hotel. He hailed a cab and ordered the coachman to drive Maggie to the Commercial, "a second class hotel."[6] Munroe, Fenety, and the unnamed remainder of their party then headed off to the American House, one of the better establishments in the city.

The next day, Munroe went to see Vail at the Commercial. The couple resumed their bickering, and Munroe left in a huff. He returned the following afternoon to tell her of his plans to leave the next morning for New York. From there, he intended to return to New Brunswick by rail, although he was careful not to share the specifics of the voyage lest she try and follow.[7] Faced with John's rejection, Maggie booked passage for herself and Ella back to Saint John.

The sojourn in Boston proved to be a milestone in the saga of Maggie and John for two reasons. The first was that Maggie adopted an alter ego during her stay, assuming the alias of Mrs. Clarke. "She was going to pass for a widow woman,"[8] Munroe later stated, a ruse to explain why a woman was travelling alone with a young child. The surname Clarke was a curious choice as the Vail family had no connection to anyone by that name. The moniker was probably suggested by Munroe, who had recently been hired to draft some designs for Mr. William Clarke in Saint John.[9]

The second revelation from their strange and strained voyage was that, contrary to Munroe's express wishes, the relationship did not end in the cut-rate Boston hotel room. Munroe had been less than truthful regarding his travel plans, for he never intended to go to New York. When Maggie boarded the steamer bound for Saint John, she immediately headed below deck to ride out the journey in tears and solitude. The instant she slipped below, John Munroe furtively made his way on board. After the ship left port, Munroe went to cunning lengths to avoid his former paramour, keeping a watchful eye on Maggie as the trip proceeded northward.[10]

Maggie did not realize she had been deceived until the boat docked in New Brunswick, and Munroe's vigilance slipped as the passengers disembarked. The couple found themselves standing face to face as they approached the gangplank. The architect simply acted as if nothing were amiss. Maggie interpreted his actions as evidence of unwavering devotion. She convinced herself he had followed her. Praying all was not lost, she reminded him she was now homeless. Munroe flagged a passing coachman, tossed the cabbie a coin, and ordered him to take her to a bargain hotel. It was, quite literally, the least he could do.

Maggie rode into the city on Friday, October 23, 1868, no longer able to deny the sorry state of her life. She was an unwed mother with no home, no money, and no family support, unable to shrug off the label of "a whore and a strumpet."[11] As the coach lurched into downtown Saint John in the early afternoon, the reality of Maggie's circumstances dawned in full measure.

Meanwhile, Munroe's hired coachman, Robert Worden, had accurately sized up the situation on the dock. He drove his charges to the Brunswick House on Prince William Street, near Reed's Point. The Brunswick had seen better days, but its proprietors struggled to maintain an air of respectability in its threadbare halls. Worden left Maggie in the coach while he went to inquire whether the Brunswick could "accommodate some ladies."[12] The mistress of the house, Mary Ann Lordly, said there were indeed vacancies. Worden fetched his passengers, delivering them to the lobby. Mrs. Lordly, hoping for a larger and more distinguished party, asked if there were more guests to come. "No," said Worden with an impish grin, and with that he slammed the door and drove off.

The driver was wise to run. The landlady surveyed her guests and did not care for what she saw. A classic battleaxe, Lordly was in no mood to be charitable. She demanded identification. Maggie revived her Boston alias, telling Lordly that "her name was Mrs. Clarke." When Lordly asked where her husband was, Maggie replied, "He had a lot of men to look after, that he was an architect, and he would not be there that night [although] he might be there to-morrow or might not."[13]

Lordly had heard it all before and trusted her intuition. She later stated, "I had my suspicions regarding Mrs. Clarke that all was not right." Even the child gave her pause. While Maggie struggled to remove her overcoat, Mrs. Lordly tried to hold Ella, but the infant erupted in tears. "It was on account of its father petting it so," Maggie said, "and it did not like to go to strangers."[14]

Accommodations were negotiated in spite of the proprietor's misgivings, and mother and child settled in for the night. A coach arrived the next morning to deliver Mrs. Clarke's trunk, a battered wooden case with no markings. Maggie and Ella kept to their room, although Maggie did ask "several times during the day if anyone had called to enquire about her checks."[15]

When the Brunswick's guests sat for supper that night, a man left a small parcel for Mrs. Clarke. The man, who refused to give his name, handed the box to another guest — a young boy named George Murray — who in turn took the package to the landlady. Mrs. Lordly interrogated the child as to the identity of the courier; George proudly declared he knew the man's name was Munroe. The packet contained a large quantity of candy, yet another mixed message for Maggie to decipher.

Other odd incidents soon followed. Just after 2:30 on Sunday morning, Mrs. Lordly noticed a bright light in Maggie's room. She entered the room to find the blinds wide open. When she went to draw them, she noticed a man standing on the street opposite, staring up at the window. Lordly kept vigil through the night as she awaited the arrival of some guests on the midnight steamer, spotting the same man passing by the hotel on at least two other occasions.

At noon on Monday, coachman Robert Worden arrived asking for Mrs. Clarke. Peering through the window, the landlady caught a glimpse of a man waiting in the hack. She recognized him as the late-night peeping Tom. Lordly demanded to know who was calling and where the coach was headed. Worden said he had Mr. John Munroe in his carriage and had been hired to take the party to Loch Lomond.

Mrs. Lordly exploded in righteous indignation. She tore up the stairs to confront Mrs. Clarke. "Look here, that man in the coach is a married man," she said, "and if he is not the father of that child I am much mistaken." Maggie met the outburst with shamed silence as Lordly told her she must never "come back to my house again."[16] Lordly then charged down to the carriage to present Munroe with a bill for services rendered. The architect handed the woman some money: $3.50 for the room and a further $1.50 for room service.[17] Maggie hastily bundled Ella into the carriage, and this thoroughly modern family drove away.

Munroe had robbed Mrs. Lordly of the last word, so she sought satisfaction elsewhere. "I had a note written and sent to John Munroe's father," she later recounted. "I told him the circumstances." His reply left her feeling equally cheated. John Sr. dismissed Mrs. Clarke as "a servant girl who had lived with his son." Although her ire was unsated, Mrs. Mary Ann Lordly would see her final command honoured. One year later, she told police she had "never seen or heard of Mrs. Clarke since."[18]

FIVE

In Sin and Error Pining

At first light, Robert Worden left his sparse room at the Union Hotel, mounted his coach, and navigated it to his usual stand on King Street, a part of town frequented by gentlemen of a loftier sort. He had just settled in when a man he knew slightly hailed him: an architect named Munroe.[1]

Munroe asked what Worden would charge to drive out to Loch Lomond. The cabbie waved off the fare, wanting no part of such a long drive on sloppy roads. The architect was undaunted, making it clear money was no object. "No matter what you charge," claimed Munroe, "it don't come out of me."[2] Worden said it would run him five dollars, an exorbitant surcharge given the journey. To Worden's chagrin, Munroe agreed. He leapt into the carriage, telling Worden to head for the Brunswick House to pick up "a friend's wife"[3] by the name of Mrs. Clarke.

Worden fetched Mrs. Clarke and her child from the hotel, although it earned him a tongue-lashing from Mrs. Lordly. The coachman seated them next to Munroe before setting off for Loch Lomond. Munroe told Worden that the lady wished to visit the Collins family, after which he and Mrs. Clarke refused all further conversation.

The previous night's rain had turned the roads into a quagmire. Worden did his best to guide the carriage to Bunker's Tavern, a journey of some three-quarters of a mile from The Forks. There, he turned right onto Black River Road and continued for another half mile. Suddenly Munroe pounded on the door of the coach. He ordered Worden to stop, saying they "would walk the rest of the way, as it was not far off."[4] While the woman carried her child toward the Collins house, Munroe asked his driver to turn the carriage around, return to Bunker's and wait until they returned. Worden followed Munroe's dictates to the letter, for he'd not yet been paid.

For the life of him, Worden could not understand why the lady agreed to walk along a muddy roadway to reach a house so readily accessible by carriage. Then again, he was a confirmed bachelor who never professed to understand a woman's mind. He turned his coach around to drive back to the public house, a trip lasting no more than ten minutes. Worden stabled his horses, ordered his lunch, and settled in to await the return of his fare.

One and a half hours passed with Worden at leisure. The cabbie finished his meal, talking rubbish with George Bunker, the twenty-one-year-old barkeep who was filling in for his uncle Horace, the publican. At two o'clock John Munroe appeared, followed shortly by Mrs. Clarke, who carried her infant daughter. Bunker offered the new arrivals something to eat or drink, but Munroe waved him off. The architect told Worden the Collins family was not at home, so Mrs. Clarke would return another time. Munroe paid Worden the agreed fare of five dollars and asked to be taken back to town immediately.[5]

Worden harnessed his team and set off for Saint John. He was annoyed to have been kept waiting with no gratuity to show for it, so he decided to have a bit of fun at his client's expense. Worden had overheard Mrs. Lordly tell Mrs. Clarke she was no longer welcome at the Brunswick House. The cabbie asked Munroe if his party would like to return to that particular hotel. John Munroe refused to take the bait, telling his driver they would not be frequenting the Brunswick "as Mrs. Clarke did not like the place."[6] He instructed Worden to take them to a hotel of his choosing, provided it was not too expensive. Realizing there was no fun to be had, Worden headed for the Union Hotel, a place he called home and knew to be moderately priced.

The coachman delivered Mrs. Clarke—who had yet to utter a sound—and her baby to the lobby of the Union. John Munroe remained in the carriage, leaving Mrs. Clarke to make her own arrangements. Worden then remounted the carriage, clucking his horses into motion. He was steering his coach past the Bell Tower at the head of King Street when Munroe again pounded the door, demanding to be let out. No more money changed hands, and "there was nothing more said."[7] Worden shook his head as he drove back to the Union, where he called it a day.

Maggie Vail was having one of those days, although the morning began with such promise. After weeks of silence from John, she had seen him standing on the street corner beneath her window late one night staring into her room. Munroe then sent the candy, along with a promise of a day's jaunt in the country.[8]

She awoke early that Monday and dressed with care, though she was still in mourning for her father and her options were limited. Protocol dictated she wear black; while it was not a colour that suited her, it lent an air of credibility to her guise as the widow Clarke. Maggie dressed Ella for a day out then sat, fidgeting anxiously, as she awaited word from her beloved John.

Even the unpleasantness with Mrs. Lordly at the Brunswick could not dampen Maggie's spirits. The weather was far from fine but nothing quelled her happiness, not even John's decision to have the coach stop in the middle of nowhere. She did not complain when he marched them through a muddy field, nor did she criticize his decision to have a picnic by the roadside or moan when no picnic materialized.[9] She said nothing when Munroe failed to visit the Collins house[10] as planned; after all, she did not know the family and was content to have John to herself. She even held her tongue when Munroe said they must walk back to Bunker's to catch their cab, a journey that ruined her skirt and shoes. She held it again when she was forced to carry Ella every step of the way. She was accustomed to suffering, perhaps even fond of it.

At the day's wistful end, Maggie found herself in the lobby of yet another boarding house. She hoped the change of location might bring better fortune, as if scandal were unable to hit a moving target. Her optimism clashed with her desolate surroundings, but she was in no position to complain.

Maggie would soon have cause to moan as she came under the scrutiny of the hotel's owner William Lake. Eggshell bald and paunchy, Lake was a textbook curmudgeon. He was also underwhelmed with his newest guest, saying, "I did not like her looks, and objected to keeping her."[11] Lake told Mrs. Clarke to move along as he was full up for the night. Fortunately for Maggie, William's word was not law at the Union Hotel. His wife Sarah shuffled out of the parlour, took a good hard look at her potential guests, and reluctantly agreed to rent Maggie a room for the week. Sarah Lake had her own doubts, later saying: "She called herself Mrs. Clarke [but] I never supposed that was her name."[12] Still, the Union Hotel was seldom found on the list of recommended tourist establishments, and desperation lowers the bar.

There was, of course, the sticky issue of payment. Mrs. Clarke assured the Lakes she was well off, claiming "she had money, about $500, property left her by her father," although she later admitted "it was gone." When asked what became of the money, Maggie replied, "her husband had it," but she insisted that "if he would only give her back her money, she would be all right."[13] William Lake balked, but his wife had a soft spot for strays. She reckoned there was a man somewhere who would pay the bill. With more than a little trepidation, Sarah Lake gave Mrs. Clarke a key and pointed her up the stairs.

Robert R. Robertson was a creature of habit. Every day he awoke at a most uncivilized hour then walked the length of Prince William Street to the door of his employer, I&F Burpee & Co., iron and hardware merchants. Robertson had served faithfully as a clerk for the past four years, sharing the counter with his colleague Henry J. Thorne. Thorne was an ambitious young man of twenty-six who would, just one year later, buy the hardware business from the Burpee brothers, Isaac and Frederick, and two decades later, serve briefly as mayor of Saint John.[14]

Although Robertson harboured no dreams of entrepreneurial fame, he had a keen eye and never forgot a face, a trait that endeared him to Burpee's clientele. He also possessed a savant-like recall of his transactions, a blessing in an era of primitive accounting. For instance, Robert Robertson clearly remembered a crisp morning in the fall of 1868 when John A. Munroe entered the premises asking to see the revolvers.[15] Munroe was a frequent visitor, someone Robertson knew by name. The clerk began laying the guns on the counter for the architect to peruse. Burpee's selection ran the gamut from single-barrelled pistols, bargain priced at $3.50, to top-of-the-line models costing upwards of $20.

Munroe considered his options, handling first one then another to get a feel for each weapon. He made small talk with Robertson as he browsed, saying he was in need of a gun at such an odd hour because he had a ticket for the boat bound for the United States that morning. The explanation was lost on the clerk as Robertson firmly believed there was no socially accepted time of day in which to purchase a firearm.[16] Minutes later, Monroe made his preference known: a Smith & Wesson .22 single barrel with seven chambers. Robertson commended the buyer on his excellent choice and set about completing the transaction.

Munroe paid cash for the gun — "either $13 or $14"; Robertson could not precisely recall — and promptly left the store to meet his waiting steamer. As Munroe hurried off into the dawn, a thought occurred to young Robertson. Though he'd seen Munroe in the store on countless occasions, the architect had never bought anything before.[17]

SIX

Forced Perspective

The morning of October 31, 1868, dawned damp and drizzly.[1] The sea released a thick fog while the ground leached rainwater, the last vestiges of a storm that had drenched the city in the days preceding. Just after nine o'clock, Robert Worden reined his team to a halt at the taxi rank on King Street, turned his collar against the cold, and searched for the day's first fare. Within minutes, the familiar silhouette of John Munroe approached the carriage. Munroe said he wanted to take the same trip as last time. Worden did not relish the idea, but the day's weather meant passengers were thin on the ground. He reluctantly agreed. Munroe did not want to leave just yet, instructing Worden to meet him at the taxi stand at eleven o'clock. From there they would fetch Mrs. Clarke and the baby.[2]

Worden did as he was bidden. Once again, Munroe remained in the carriage as Worden retrieved Mrs. Clarke and her daughter before heading toward Loch Lomond. The trek passed in silence. Worden later said, "I do not recollect him speaking to me from the time we started until we got to the same place on Black River Road."[3]

The near-record rainfalls of the past week left the roads rutted and slick, and it was half past twelve before the coach passed by Bunker's Tavern.[4] At precisely the same location as the previous journey, Munroe hammered his fist on the carriage door. Worden slowed to a halt. Munroe jumped from the coach while the woman struggled with the infant, who'd grown into a hefty eight-month-old. When Worden turned the carriage about, he "looked back, and saw them walking along the road — she was carrying the child."[5] Munroe and Mrs. Clarke were on opposite sides of the lane. Not a look or word passed between them. Worden signalled his horses and headed for the tavern, leaving them to their lovers' quarrel.

It was one o'clock before Worden arrived at Bunker's Tavern. He fed and watered his horses before turning his thoughts to his own stomach. He ordered a substantial lunch, settling into the taproom to await his food. Worden was a garrulous raconteur, and he regaled George Bunker, who once again manned the bar, with the miseries of his journey.

No more than forty minutes later, Munroe walked into the saloon, doffed his hat — "a half-beaver" in the latest style — and wiped his sweaty brow. Munroe was alone. Bunker noted "his face appeared somewhat red, like a man who had been walking fast." Munroe told Worden he was ready to go. The coachman told him to hold his horses, as he had not yet received his lunch. Munroe again told Worden "he was in a hurry" and could not wait.[6] Worden asked young Bunker how long it would be before his dinner was ready and was told it would be a few minutes.[7] Finding the answer satisfactory, Worden settled back into his seat.

Clearly he did not realize the tenacity of his opponent. Munroe came undone, growling through clenched teeth that it did "not make any difference"[8] how fast the meal might be served, he wanted to leave immediately. He then threw money at the problem, promising to pay for the coachman's food but only if they returned to the city that instant. Worden abandoned his dream of a hot lunch and went to ready the horses.

Munroe followed Worden to the door. He stopped short at the threshold, insisting he wanted to pay his fare. Worden informed Munroe the trip would cost him six dollars this time, awarding himself punitive damages for his mental anguish and suffering. Munroe handed the hack a series of bills and a mild kerfuffle ensued regarding the change. With his account finally reconciled, Munroe dismissed Worden to ready the coach while he returned to the bar.

Munroe again mopped his clammy brow as he ordered a brandy. Before he downed his drink, Munroe asked how much he owed for the liquor and the cabbie's untouched lunch. Bunker told him the tab was one dollar.

Munroe drank up, pulled a bill from his pocket, tossed it on the bar, and then stormed toward the stables. The overt rudeness of the supposedly gentrified class never ceased to amaze the barman. Bunker picked up the glass and the bill before heading behind the bar. Only then did he notice Munroe had left a two-dollar bill.[9]

Out in the stables, Worden barely had time to bridle his horses when Munroe lunged for the carriage door, anxious to be away. Worden asked if they should wait for the woman and child to join them, but Munroe insisted "that Mr. Collins would drive her in to the boat" when she was finished visiting with the family.[10] Worden resigned himself to silence and pointed the carriage for home.

The minute the carriage lurched into motion, John Munroe visibly relaxed. Apropos of nothing, he began to recount intimate stories of his childhood, which he shouted at a bewildered Worden. Munroe's reminiscences suggested he knew the road quite well. He began narrating a curious travelogue for Worden's benefit. "He showed me where he used to live," Worden later stated. "[I] didn't know the old Munroe place till he showed me."[11] Prompted by the passing landmarks, Munroe extolled the virtues of long-lost neighbours or the glories of a particular boyhood fishing hole. Worden simply grunted and prayed for the lights of Saint John.

The return trip lasted nearly two hours. As Worden finally crested the hill and began the descent into the city centre, Munroe asked to be let out on Prince William Street, claiming "he had business there."[12] He asked Worden to collect Mrs. Clarke's trunk from the Union Hotel and take it to the boat bound for America on Monday morning, claiming that she was heading to Boston and would not return to the hotel. It was all too much information for Worden. Munroe also told the coachman to have the trunk on the dock by Monday's first light, promising he would meet him there. Before Worden could get a word in edgewise, Munroe vanished into the fog. Worden sat for a moment in stunned silence. He had never encountered a man quite like John Munroe. He made a mental note to ask a fellow driver to deal with the trunk, and then he headed for home.

All Hallows' Eve of 1868 passed with little fanfare in the home of Phileanor Crear. It had been months since she last saw Maggie — the second day of August to be exact. She was worried, although not enough to report her sister's disappearance to the proper authorities. Still, she could not shake the persistent vexation scratching at the back of her mind, a sense that all was not right.

Christmas came and went, but there was still no word from Maggie. Reports of the occasional sighting continued to trickle in. For instance, James Reynolds, a tailor who lived on Germain Street, claimed he saw Maggie "looking out of the window of some house as he passed." Philly asked William Irvine, a painter from Carleton, to investigate. When Irvine inquired at the house in question, he was told Maggie "had left and gone to the States with John Munroe."[13] Maggie's twenty-fourth birthday passed without celebration; her daughter Ella May's first birthday went unfeted. Winter thawed into spring, and spring warmed into summer, and all the while the itch in Phileanor's head grew stronger.

Philly travelled to Saint John for a brief visit with her mother-in-law during the first week of June 1869. She was strolling along King Street when she caught a glimpse of John Munroe.[14] She ran toward him as he made a sudden turn and darted off in the opposite direction. Philly gave chase but soon lost him in a crowd. She spent the next few days searching for the wayward architect but never found him.

Phileanor left Saint John on June 9, travelling onward to Carleton.[15] She lingered for a week, calling on family and gazing wistfully at her ancestral home on Lancaster Road. The house dredged up thoughts of Maggie that passed through Philly's mind like a funeral cortège. She despaired of ever seeing her sister again.

On June 17, Phileanor made her way along the harbour front, where she passed the postmaster, Mr. Reed. Although she had not lived in Carleton for some time, Philly's face was still a familiar one. Reed stopped her short, asking if her name was now Crear. When she said it was, Reed announced, "I have a letter that was left for you to-day, particular."[16] She accompanied Reed to the post office, where he dispatched an errand boy to retrieve the letter.

Philly stared at the envelope, for she did not recognize the handwriting. Although it was hand delivered, it arrived with no postage due, a fact she confirmed twice with Mr. Reed. The envelope bore multiple earmarks: a three-cent American stamp as well as postmarks from "Boston, Mass.," "St. John, N.B.," and a final imprint from "Carleton, St. John."[17] The postmaster deciphered the codes, assuring Philly the letter was first mailed in Boston.

Philly pocketed the envelope and quickly made her way to the home of her sister-in-law Mary Crear, the only literate person she knew. Mary Crear drew the note from the envelope and read the following:

> Dear File,
> i swore i woud never let you know how i got on but i am
> going to cicago in a few days. My Husband a Painter has
> got a year's work. i am gone to have another in October the
> first of the Month. i am getting on bully. when i get over i
> may come on in the spring, i told him i was a widder. He is
> teaching me to write. i have wrote to John before. we are all
> well May is well.
>
> Mrs. Maggie Crandall[18]

Mary Crear asked Philly who might have sent the letter, having no personal acquaintance with anyone named Crandall. She wondered whether it could be from Philly's long-lost sister, since the Christian name was Margaret. Phileanor dismissed the possibility, but only because she "did not want them to know that [Maggie] had a child."[19] She thanked Mary for her help and headed for home.

Philly hid the letter, never showing it to her husband or any other member of her family. Her search for Maggie and Ella ended the day it arrived. She had all the information she needed. The itching in her brain was gone.

SEVEN

Into the Woods

On Tuesday, September 7, 1869, the citizens of Saint John turned out in record numbers to welcome a most regal guest: His Royal Highness Prince Arthur. Rumoured to be Victoria's favourite son, Arthur William Patrick Albert was also the darling of the Maritime media. The prince, all of nineteen and a lieutenant in the Rifle Brigade, was midway through an eight-week tour of Canada.[1]

In Saint John, every ship mast flew the colours and bunting dripped from lampposts. Although the eyes of the city were fixed on the harbour front, those in the outlying boroughs went about their days, business as usual. With little thought for the royal pageantry downtown, a small band of "coloured girls and young men,"[2] gathered on the road leading to Willow Grove near Loch Lomond. Their destination was a series of marshy flats known locally as Blueberry Plain. As the name implied, their task for the day was berry picking. The group included three sets of sisters: Martha, Caroline, and Margaret Thompson; Susan and Jemima Lane; and Mary and Susan Corbyn. Their escorts were four unrelated men: George Diggs, Prince Fowler, Henry Brandy, and Isaiah Gabels.[3] No one in the group was old enough to vote, a moot point as the right to do so would not be granted to women or those of African descent for decades to come.

While the sun burned off the last of the morning cloud, the Thompson girls settled in a promising patch just off Black River Road. Martha worked through the best bushes then broke from the group to explore farther afield, pushing aside some low-lying branches. She glimpsed a flash of white on the ground, spying what looked like a row of teeth. Shocked, she tumbled onto her backside, bellowing for her sisters.[4] Margaret and Caroline ran to her side with Prince Fowler and George Diggs close behind. Martha pointed to the brush, shrieking something about a head. Diggs grabbed a stick and began poking about. He soon discovered a human skull, complete with its jaw and a thick braid of long brown hair. Clearing away the brush, Diggs found a pile of clothes and a hoop skirt, as well as some additional bones. Using the stick to dig through the moss, he found a child's shoe with a stocking attached. Tiny bones rattled inside.

What happened next depends on who was telling the story.[5] The women claimed they were frightened by what they saw and wanted to get help, but the men told them not to say a word to anyone. The men later denied that, saying the decision to remain mum was unanimous. The lone point of consensus was that the discovery was made at three that afternoon and the group left the area just after four o'clock. The berry-pickers left the skull and bones where they lay, but they did not head straight for home, a decision they would come to regret. Instead, they beat a leisurely, circuitous path back to the road, stopping frequently to pick more fruit.

The oath of secrecy sworn on Blueberry Plain did not last the night. Caroline Thompson was barely through the door when she told her mother and father of the gruesome find.[6] Susan Lane kept her vow only a few minutes longer, telling her father that same evening.[7] From then, the news radiated throughout the community: Susan's father told a man named Kennedy, who in turn told his wife, who then told William Douglas, the first white man to hear the tale. By week's end, it seemed everyone knew of the bones out on Black River Road.

William Douglas was a farmer, a lifelong resident of Willow Grove and as pragmatic a man as ever drew breath. On Sunday, September 12, Douglas reassembled the band of berry-pickers and insisted they show him the body.[8] The group remained silent, staring at the ground as though the answer were written there. Douglas turned to George Diggs and demanded to be taken to the site. According to Douglas, "It was some time before he made an answer; at length, he said he knew nothing about

FIG. 3 An enterprising souvenir salesman produced a postcard featuring the "coloured girls and young men" re-enacting the moment they discovered the remains. Note the poorly rendered skull and bones added for effect.

it." Henry Brandy rose to Diggs's defence, but George told him to "hush up and say no more about it."[9] Before the whole thing came to blows, Douglas let the matter drop.

He tried again the next day, this time focusing his efforts on the female pickers. A few, including Mary Corbyn, reluctantly agreed to show him the remains, and they headed out to the plain. No more than forty yards off the road, Douglas found the bones, clothing, and hair. Mary grabbed a stick and flipped the skull over, bringing with it a rotting piece of a woman's bonnet: "Out of it ran brains and stuff, making a great smell."[10]

As the party surveyed the scene, a second neighbourhood delegation arrived. Two of the road's resident busybodies, Miss Sarah Collins and Mrs. Porter, had heard whispers of the bones and came to see for themselves. Douglas warned the women of the noxious sights beyond, but they forged into the woods undeterred.

Douglas returned home to prepare a letter for the authorities in Saint John. He was unable to mail it that Monday, however, having missed the

last stagecoach for town, and farm obligations prevented him from send-
ing it on Tuesday. On Wednesday morning he drove to the city, where he
met with the police magistrate, Constable Powers, and the coroner, Dr.
Sylvester Earle. Douglas guided officials back to the site, where "they
gathered up the remains and brought them away."[11]

The sudden appearance of uniformed men on the shores of Loch
Lomond piqued the interest of the local media, who began sniffing around
the plain. Reporters soon learned of the berry-pickers' activities, and the
teens came under harsh scrutiny. "Like frightened children they fled from
the scene,"[12] the *St. John Daily Telegraph and Morning Journal* declared.
The editors were outraged to discover the youths had paused to pick more
berries as they retreated. Another publication chastised the group for
leaving the remains as found, saying the choice displayed "their utter
ignorance of the demands of humanity."[13]

Condemnation fell hardest on Henry Brandy, faintly praised as "the
most intelligent"[14] of the lot. He and Diggs were soon labelled as the
masterminds of some sordid plot, their alleged crimes ranged from
murdering the unknown victim to grave robbing. The latter accusation
found traction thanks to a report in which "it is stated, but not proved,
that a broach [*sic*] and locket were found on the spot some time ago."[15]
The misguided oath of secrecy was seen as evidence of guilt; the press
could find no other reason why Diggs and Brandy had sworn the others
to silence. Despite the harping of the fourth estate, the male berry-pickers
were never formally considered suspects. The remains had clearly been
there for some time, although just how long no one could yet say for sure.
Police also questioned how many bodies were present, and whether the
person or persons unknown had succumbed to the cold or ill health, had
chosen an isolated spot in which to commit suicide, or had met with foul
play.

The answer to one of those questions came quickly. When the coroner
examined the scene, he noticed the largest sections of brush covering the
remains were cut from trees in the area. Comparisons of the severed ends
matched perfectly. Investigators also noted sizable patches of moss had
been torn up and used to cover the remains, forming a shallow but

unmistakable grave. The coroner announced that suicide and natural causes could be ruled out, as the dead cannot bury themselves.

A second riddle was answered when the local publican, Horace Bunker, thinking it "strange" that "more of the bones were not found," decided to search the grounds surrounding the clandestine grave shortly after the coroner's visit; John March, a journalist, accompanied him. Within minutes, Bunker noticed "the skull of a child, about six or seven yards from where the remains of the woman were found." He called for March, who gathered up the friable bones, wrapped them in newspaper, and transported the lot to the coroner's office. Although a child's boot and stocking had already been found in the vicinity, investigators had recovered no further evidence of a younger decedent. They naively hoped the shoe was simply an anomaly. After March bore the infant skull back to town, authorities could no longer deny there were at least two victims.[16]

Confirmation of a dead child ignited a firestorm in the press, and in the absence of hard facts, speculation ran rampant. Reporters envisioned countless scenarios to explain the strange scene; many elected to print conjecture as established truth. Among the most lurid were the musings of the *St. John Daily Telegraph and Morning Journal*:

> The party was probably driving along the road together, the intending murderer perhaps helping to beguile the time by pleasant words. It was the dark of night — a place suitable to the deed was found. The murderer's arm was raised. The well-aimed fatal shot was fired and the young mother is numbered among the dead. The murderous passion is further indulged, and the easy task of despatching the child is speedily accomplished.[17]

The *Telegraph* waxed on, packing more scandalized outrage into a single paragraph than its less erudite competitors thought possible. The paper's editors could not imagine "a darker or more atrocious deed of blood" than "the perpetration of two murders of appalling atrocity," and they prayed that some clue "may yet lead to the discovery of the black-hearted and cowardly murderer," drawing strength from the knowledge that "though he is still unknown, facts are accumulating which may yet enable the officers of justice to say to the murderer, 'thou art the man!'"[18]

While the press focused on the as-yet-unnamed perpetrator, officials set their sights on the still-unidentified victims. With nothing more than some bones and a few scraps of clothing to guide them, identifying the remains seemed an insurmountable task.

ACT TWO

In which questions of character help to unmask a killer,
or lead investigators on a wild goose chase.

EIGHT

Ashes and Dust

Saint John city coroner Sylvester Earle was a trained physician, a rarity in a time when a medical licence was not a prerequisite to conduct autopsies. The son of a doctor, Earle studied medicine at the University of the City of New York, earning his degree in 1844. After graduation, he made the obligatory grand tour of Europe, calling in at hospitals in the major capitals to observe the latest innovations. Earle returned to New Brunswick in 1845 to join his father's practice and was appointed coroner in 1867.[1]

After assuming jurisdiction of the case, Earle ordered the collection of all visible bones and clothing from Black River Road. The materials were delivered to "the dead house," a precursor of the city morgue.[2] Although entirely capable of conducting an autopsy himself, Earle recognized he had limited experience with decomposed bodies, and he directed his friend and colleague Dr. James Christie to examine the remains.

Christie was one of Saint John's less conventional practitioners, eschewing a traditional hospital appointment to open a surgery in his home at the corner of Dorchester and Union Streets.[3] Although the city's charnel house was just around the block, Christie opted to take the remains home to perform a more thorough examination, much to the chagrin of his wife and neighbours.[4]

The smell was the least of his problems, for the condition of the bodies left Christie little to examine. Animals had scavenged the flesh beyond all recognition. The scraps of clothing were rusted with blood and annealed with desiccated tissue. What remained of the adult now fit inside a lady's hatbox, while the last vestiges of the child nestled easily in the palm of the doctor's hand.[5]

Dr. LeBaron Botsford followed the telltale stench to the corner of Dorchester and Union to offer Christie his assistance. "My curiosity brought me there," Botsford later explained, and Christie was happy to have him. LeBaron was an old-school family doctor who had practised medicine for thirty-four years. He was more experienced than Christie when it came to suspicious deaths.[6]

The two men began their examination with the adult skull, as "it was the only thing that was perfect; the other bones were in a great measure destroyed." After cleaning the cranium, Christie "found a circular aperture in the left temple; on measuring it, it proved to be a quarter and a sixteenth of an inch in diameter." Upon closer inspection, the entrance wound bore "traces of lead where the ball entered."[7] The fragments were visible to the naked eye and readily apparent with a magnifying lens. Christie "sawed off the top of the skull to get a good view of the interior" and better determine the trajectory.[8] The bullet had blown a much larger hole through the inner table of bone, a clear indication of the projectile's direction of travel. Christie believed the death was caused by the bullet severing the "meningen"[9] artery, concluding: "I have no doubt but the person to whom this skull belonged was shot by a pistol bullet...of very small size."[10]

Christie returned to Black River Road later that afternoon determined to find the offending bullet. He sifted through the rancid patch of ground where the skull was discovered and "among the brain matter [he] found a small fragment of the inner table of the skull."[11] When he brought the fragment home, it fit perfectly into the wound. Despite repeated searches of the area, however, no bullet was recovered.

Back in Christie's surgery, he and Botsford shared their thoughts as to the identity of the decedents. "I could not tell by the skull the sex of the person,"[12] Christie stated, although the long braid and feminine attire led him to conclude the adult was female. Based on the recovered clothing, the physicians thought the woman occupied "a respectable social position."[13] Based on the "condition of her teeth, which are not much worn, and the softness of her bones"[14] as well as "the acuteness of the ridges

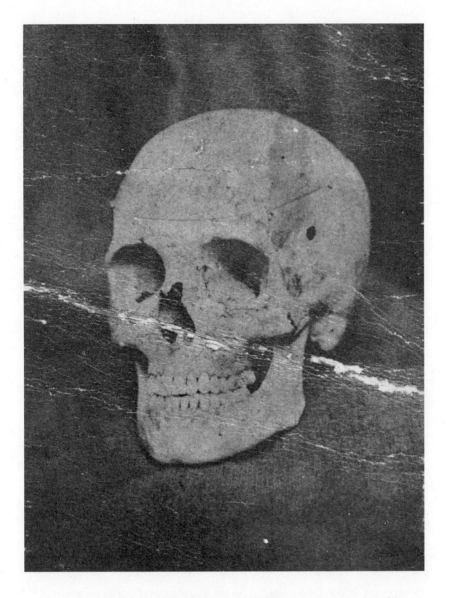

FIG. 4 The skull of the adult victim with the entrance wound visible
to the left temple. The image was reproduced as a souvenir postcard,
widely distributed during the subsequent trial.

in the skull,"[15] Christie estimated her age to be twenty to twenty-five; Botsford thought the skull belonged to "a person over thirty years of age."[16] He later hedged when pressed to elaborate, stating, "I don't care about saying anything about the age."[17]

As for the juvenile remains, Christie offered an age estimate based on a lone molar recovered at the crime scene. He opined the child was "twelve to fourteen months" though, he conceded, "it might have been older."[18] Later, during an interview with the *St. John Daily Telegraph and Morning Journal*, he amended his estimate to eighteen months.[19] The infant's gender was listed as undetermined, as Christie "made no discovery by which [he] could distinguish the sex of the child."[20] Botsford wanted no part in guessing the sex or age of the juvenile remains.[21] If experience had taught him anything, it was to recognize his own limitations.

To placate the public's growing fears, the press was quick to put distance between newspaper readers and the tragedy. Editors assured the masses that "as no mother or child has been missed in this community we may infer that the blood which pollutes our land is that of strangers."[22] The *Telegraph* further postulated the victims must have been from the States, a feeble hypothesis grounded only in the style of the woman's fashions.

Although the adult's cause of death was readily apparent, both Christie and Botsford refused to offer any opinion as to how the child met its untimely end. The press, however, showed no such reticence. On September 20, 1869, the *Telegraph* stated the still-unnamed fiend had "strangled the child to which he may have been bound by the nearest ties of blood!" How the reporter reached such a conclusion was not stipulated. According to police, the relationship between the two victims was still unknown, much less their familial connection to the killer. The only purpose such unsubstantiated claims served was to fuel public outrage, putting unprecedented pressure on the coroner and police to solve this mystery.

On Thursday, September 16, 1869, Sylvester Earle convened an inquest into the unnatural deaths on Black River Road. The proceedings were open to the public yet failed to draw a crowd, although a "number of medical men, members of the press and others were present."[23]

Earle ascended a bench at the county courthouse normally reserved for the province's Supreme Court justices. He began by selecting his jury. A seven-man panel was quickly sworn and seated: James Crawford, George Scribner, James Green, Lewis W. Durant, William Crabs, William R. Russell, and John Daly, who was elected foreman.[24] At that time jurors were required to witness the autopsy in cases of suspicious death, but protocol was abandoned because of the bodies' decomposed state; Earle elected instead to bring the bones into court. The smell arrived well in advance of the actual remains, forcing jurors to cover their faces with handkerchiefs. The stench also may have contributed to the unusually poor attendance in the courtroom that day.

Earle then called each of the berry-pickers who discovered the bodies, beginning with Martha Thompson and her sisters, Caroline and Margaret. In the official inquest transcript, their testimony is headed by their names along with the disclaimer "[colored]," a label which simultaneously explained and dismissed the testimony that followed. The females collectively held to their version of events, claiming the men ordered them into silence. Diggs and Brandy then took the stand and contradicted their story. Repeated questioning regarding the missing locket and brooch elicited nothing but denials and obfuscation.

The testimony of the day's lone white witness, William Douglas, drove home the suspicious actions of the berry-pickers. He spoke of the teens' reluctance to return to the crime scene as well as their refusal to answer his questions. Of course, the youths were completely within their rights to ignore Douglas, who was simply a farmer with no civic authority. His indignation reflected the persistent social belief that blacks still answered to whites despite the formal demise of slavery decades earlier.

Douglas's appearance also highlighted a major weakness inherent in all coroner inquests. In 1869, as now, a coroner has jurisdictional authority to subpoena witnesses and compel testimony, yet there is little the coroner can do with witnesses who appear but refuse to cooperate. The berry-pickers surrendered themselves to the court as ordered, answering the questions put to them. That no one liked their answers was unfortunate, but not illegal. If they didn't want to talk, the coroner couldn't make them. This cast a spotlight on another curious flaw in the system: at that particular moment in Canada's history, the coroner's authority to interrogate witnesses exceeded that of the police.[25] As a result, the paltry contributions of the berry-pickers were as good as they would get.

By late afternoon, Earle had exhausted his finite pool of eyewitnesses, making no discernible headway. With the weekend looming, he adjourned the inquest until two p.m. on Monday, September 20. The coroner had bought himself ninety-six hours to ponder his options—plenty of time had he known where all this was heading, but nowhere near long enough for a man without a clue what to do next.

NINE

Raising Cain

Indiantown had seen its fortunes fluctuate like the tides of its most famous landmark, the Reversing Falls. In its prime the area boasted a population of over 2,500, mostly unemployed labourers drawn by the riverboats docked in the undulating harbour. The region earned its name from a trading post erected in the late 1770s on what is now Bridge Street. At some point the post "was turned over to the Indians [and] became known as 'Indian House,'"[1] later amended to Indiantown as its population swelled.

At the corner of Main and Peters Streets stood James Cain's grocery store.[2] Its proprietor had emigrated from Ireland, opening his modest shop with visions of prosperity in the New World. The dream had yet to materialize, but Cain was undaunted. The recent addition of alcohol to the store's shelves increased foot traffic, allowing Cain to take on his son as a partner. James Jr. lacked his father's immigrant gumption, but he had a wife to support and few marketable skills, so he reluctantly joined his father behind the counter.

On Saturday, September 18, 1869, James Jr. was minding his business when a local constable entered the shop. The cop informed Cain that the police magistrate, Justice Tapley, wanted to see him. When asked why, the officer said Cain needed "to explain a statement made by his aunt."[3] The aunt in question, Mary Cain, had recently fallen out with rest of the Cain clan, a situation made all the more awkward by her refusal to leave the family home above the store.[4]

James Cain followed the constable to the "commodious"[5] Italianate home of police magistrate David Tapley. Judge Tapley divided his time among his various vocations and avocations: lumber surveyor, politician, lawyer, and justice of the civil court of Portland, a parish on the outskirts of Saint John. Tapley was everything Cain was not: wealthy, formidable, and politically connected. The only things Cain had going for him were his Irish temper and a marked disdain for authority.

Despite his political clout, Tapley was on shaky ground. The judge had summoned Cain to address rumours of the grocer's extramarital activities, stories that Tapley had heard from his wife. Normally he would not concern himself with such base gossip, but the drama unfolding at the coroner's inquest had the entire city on edge. Everyone wanted to know the identity of the murdered woman and child. Thanks to the scurrilous gossip, Tapley harboured a sneaking suspicion Cain knew something.

Tapley began the interview cordially, assuring Cain he was not under arrest — at least, not yet. The judge then recounted the rumours being spread by Mary Cain. She had told a number of people that while Cain was "a soldier in the southern army,"[6] he had married a woman down in New Orleans. When his tour of duty ended, he returned to New Brunswick without his war bride. According to Mary, as Cain re-established himself in Indiantown, a local beauty turned his head; she became his second wife. The couple set up house above the family business on Main Street, a home they shared with Mary Cain and several others.[7]

The situation took an opprobrious turn in the fall of 1868 when the New Orleans war bride arrived in Indiantown with a child in tow and began pounding on Cain's front door.[8] Those who saw the woman described her as "good-looking," swathed in a form-fitting green dress with a luxurious mane of brown hair that "hung in dingles."[9] Mary said the current Mrs. Cain was none too pleased with this unexpected development, and "it made [for] considerable talk among the neighbors."[10] According to those neighbours, James Cain "came to the door and [the woman] recognized him, but he did not know her," or so Mary Cain claimed. The woman scorned then went back to the carriage. She lifted her child aloft, shouting: "If you don't know me, don't you know your child?"[11] Cain forcefully denied the child as well. Wife number one then drew a piece of paper from her pocket—reportedly their marriage licence—and waved it at her amnesiac husband, asking if he remembered signing the form. Despite Mary Cain's best efforts at eavesdropping, she could not hear his mumbled reply.[12]

The standoff lasted several minutes, ample time for Mary Cain and a few select neighbours to grab front row seats to the spectacle. When the marriage bond failed to elicit the desired response, the first Mrs. Cain conceded defeat, and "the same coach that brought them to the door took them away again."[13] The confrontation ended as quickly as it began, although everyone within earshot thought James Cain still had a lot of explaining to do.

Once the carriage pulled away, tongues wagged as to the fate of Cain's southern family. Mary Cain told her neighbours the family was taking up a collection "to pacify that woman," using the funds to house James's illegitimate family at a hotel in town until the matter could be resolved. Mary said the woman and child ended up at the Brunswick House, the only boarding house willing to harbour such a scandal-soaked party.[14]

Having recounted the sordid tale, Judge Tapley asked James Cain if he had anything to say in response to the allegations made against him. Cain was first dumbstruck and then "indignant,"[15] vehemently denying the entire affair. He also had a few choice words for his aunt, and for any neighbour who repeated her bilious rubbish. Cain's umbrage failed to move the judge. Tapley issued a writ remanding Cain into the custody of the local constables, who transported him to the lock-up in the city centre. Confident he had fulfilled his duty, the judge again put pen to paper, drafting a brief letter to his fellow police magistrate in Saint John and addressing a copy to the coroner. Tapley outlined the evidence to date and wished them all the luck in the world.

The authorities in Saint John received the arrest of James Cain and the information in Tapley's letter with hearty praise—and more than a little relief. It seemed the mystery of Black River Road would be solved in no time, or so they believed right up until the moment a coroner's investigator met a coachman named Robert Worden.

✠

For the second time that week, Sylvester Earle found himself in a carriage hurtling toward Black River Road. At his side sat the chief of police. Sequestered in the seat behind was Robert Worden. It was Sunday, September 19, 1869.

It had been an eventful morning. Earle had planned to use the remainder of the weekend to patch the holes in Cain's account before concluding his inquest on Monday. To that end, he sent one of his investigators by the Brunswick House to gather any information that might help identify the victims. Things had not gone according to plan.

Joseph Lordly was quite forthcoming about two particular guests—a young woman who called herself Mrs. Clarke, and her infant daughter—but they were not from New Orleans. Furthermore, Lordly had never heard of James Cain. He did, however, recall a man named Munroe who had shown more than a passing interest in Mrs. Clarke and her child. Lordly sent the investigator to see the coachman Robert Worden, suggesting he might know more. The coroner's deputy found Worden sitting in his hack. He willingly followed the deputy to the central office for questioning.

Earle and the police chief sat transfixed as Worden told of his multiple sojourns out to Loch Lomond. They paid special interest to Worden's description of how Munroe had returned without his escorts during the second journey. The coroner insisted Worden take him to the exact location where the coach stopped.

As the police wagon sped along Black River Road, Earle planned to "drive Worden past the spot" as a test of the coachman's memory and honesty. When the carriage drew near the crime scene, Worden signalled the driver to halt. He recalled the precise point he had "put them out of his coach,"[16] a location directly adjacent to the clandestine gravesite.

The coachman's story withstood scrutiny, leaving Earle with a quandary. James Cain already stood accused of the crime, and yet it seemed John Munroe might also have blood on his hands. Two adulterous men, two wanton women, two illegitimate children—which story was the coroner to believe? Earle decided to be cautious and issue a subpoena for Munroe, although he ordered it be served with civility and discretion.

In a plot twist found only in pulp fiction and real life, the warrant was erroneously issued in the name of George Munroe, John's younger sibling.[17] Exactly how the mix-up occurred was not recorded for posterity, although it likely stemmed from Worden's inability to distinguish between the brothers. The constables dispatched to George Munroe's home soon learned they had the wrong Munroe.

News travels fast in a city the size of Saint John, and it was not long before the right Munroe heard of his brother's brush with the law. John Munroe did not rush to George's aid, opting instead to head straight to his lawyer's office.[18] That lawyer was Samuel R. Thomson, a high-priced and much-sought-after barrister recently appointed as Queen's Counsel. Munroe, visibly flustered and understandably concerned, arrived at Thomson's august Hazen Street home-cum-law-office just as the Thomsons were sitting down to dinner. Thomson apologized to his wife and directed his client to his study.[19] The leather-bound souvenirs of his well-rounded education lined the room, a workplace designed to instill trust. Munroe was instantly calmed. Surrounded by the trappings of wealth and privilege, the two men hunkered down over brandies and strategized for hours. After hearing Munroe's story, Thomson advised his client to present himself to the coroner for questioning. Munroe did not care for that option, but Thomson convinced him it was in his best interest.

Munroe's decision to hire Thomson was an inspired one. Both men were ambitious, more than a little arrogant, and well respected. Thomson knew how to handle men like Munroe—after all, they were cut from the same cloth—and his influence over his client was masterful. He could not hope to contain Munroe's ego or emotion, but he could use them in his favour. For example, Munroe would later tell reporters that while "he had placed himself in the hands of the Coroner" at his lawyer's insistence, such a voluntary surrender was very much "in accordance with his own inclination."[20] Thomson achieved his desired outcome by making it seem as if it were all Munroe's idea. Even in his darkest hour, appearances were everything to men like Munroe.

TEN

What Fresh Hell

A discernibly larger crowd funnelled into the coroner's inquest on the afternoon of Monday, September 20, 1869. Even so, those in the gallery were not expecting much. Word of James Cain's arrest had not leaked to the press, and they had yet to hear the name John Munroe. There was no trace of either man in the courtroom or any sign of the weekend's developments. For all the spectators knew, the parade of berry-pickers would pick up exactly where it left off, which is precisely what happened.

At two o'clock, Sylvester Earle called his inquest to order. First to the stand was the last of the pickers, Jemima Lane, who added nothing of substance to the case narrative.[1] After a very brief appearance by Jane Davidson,[2] a spinster from Willow Grove who swore she saw nothing of relevance, the gallery grew restless. All indications were the inquest would end with a pile of unidentified bones and an unsolvable mystery.

Next in the dock was a raftsman and lumber driver from Portland named Samuel Peters.[3] The crowd groaned when he announced he "knew nothing about this affair until yesterday morning."[4] Just as the correspondent from the *Saint John Daily Morning News* decided to go off in search of a real story, he noticed all of the coroner's questions to Peters related to a man by the name of James Cain.[5] The reporter reclaimed his seat and drew his notepad as Peters began to share the intimate details of Cain's infidelities. Peters became the story's de facto narrator, introducing a strange cast of characters to the court: the beautiful but scorned mistress and her ill-gotten progeny, the clueless wife, and the loud-mouthed aunt who had told him the entire tale.

Peters regaled the now rapt audience with all the sordid (if sometimes vague) details, including how Cain's American family had fled in tears from the village when the grocer "would not receive them." Samuel seemed to relish his moment of notoriety, growing more animated with each question. He even placed himself in the centre of the action: when asked if he'd brought the scandal to Cain's attention, Peters replied: "I told Kane [*sic*] about it and he denied it." Peters stepped down from the witness dock with his conscience scrubbed clean. He had done his civic duty, betraying his neighbour's secrets in the interests of justice. If it occurred to Peters that the price Cain might pay for his brutal honesty was death, it clearly did not bother him.[6]

Peters's testimony had awakened the lethargic throng, but the next witness brought them to the edge of their seats. Mary Cain made her boisterous and laboured way to the dock, carping *sotto voce* the entire way. The very definition of a hostile witness, she wanted no part of these proceedings. She was well cast in the role. She was unmarried and her genetics conspired to keep her that way. She was as bitter as day-old coffee and had grown abusive in her dotage, sustained only by her need to castigate the family she simultaneously lived with and shunned.[7]

Mary took the stand and proclaimed every last man, woman, and child in Indiantown a liar. "I never told Samuel Peters or any other person such a thing," she screeched. "I never told George Dunham . . . Jacob Pidgeon, Charles Cowan, Stephen Shaw, Police Magistrate or anyone else, anything of the kind." Instead, she pointed a gnarled finger at Samuel Peters, swearing it was he who asked her if she'd seen the woman. Being the good Christian sort, she could not tell a lie and felt duty bound to confirm she "had heard such a report but never saw any woman." She also did not recall saying that "money must be raised to pacify that woman."[8]

Mary's performance was electrifying for the same reason it was easily dismissed: the woman simply protested too much. Her denials were too pat and her knowledge of events too detailed to support her contention that she "did not start these rumours . . . and never heard James or his father say anything about it."[9] The *Daily Morning News* devoted two days of coverage to dissecting her testimony.[10] It was not a flattering analysis.

With Mary Cain's caterwauls still ringing in his ears, the coroner called to the stand several residents of Indiantown's Main Street as rebuttal witnesses. George Dunham raised his right hand and swore Mary Cain was the liar. Dunham, a lumber dealer in the parish of Portland, told the court that exactly one year ago to the day, he was passing along Main Street when Mary Cain accosted him. "She asked me if I had heard the news,"[11] Dunham recalled. When he asked what news, she proceeded to lay out the entire ordeal in exhaustive detail.

James Williams, a Portland-area painter, replaced Dunham on the stand. Williams had not only heard Mary Cain's version of events but also shared a coach with Cain's alleged first wife. In the fall of 1868, Williams was returning from Boston. The final leg of his journey found him in a public carriage bound for Indiantown. He struck up a conversation with a fellow passenger. The young man, smirking from ear to ear, asked Williams if he had seen Jimmy Cain's wife. Williams replied he had not, stating that as far as he knew Cain's wife was tending the store as usual. The young man whispered, "This is another wife" and pointed to a woman sitting with her child in the ladies' cabin of the coach.[12]

James Williams was not the only one to have seen the mysterious southern bride. James E. Sprague was a teamster who lived across from the Cains on Main Street. Sprague was driving his truck "up the hill at Indiantown with a load of market produce" when he encountered a carriage standing idle in front of Cain's storefront. "The coach being in my way I had to stop," Sprague said, placing him at an ideal vantage point to witness the exchange between Cain and his ersatz wife. Sprague also told the coroner: "At different times during the winter, Mary Kane [*sic*] stated the same things to me that I saw myself." Mary had committed a cardinal sin of gossiping: rehashing a story to someone who was actually there. Sprague swore Mary told him "they had to pay the woman's board in the city." With that, Sprague stepped down.[13]

Sylvester Earle had heard enough. He needed time to sort out the latest findings and to figure out if or how John Munroe fit in. He adjourned the inquest until Thursday afternoon and ordered the bailiff to make arrangements to transport the jurors to Black River Road the following day, allowing the panel to examine the crime scene first-hand.

The coroner may have harboured some doubt as to Cain's involvement, but the day's testimony convinced at least one man of his guilt: Andrew Wetmore, the attorney general. Wetmore ordered that Cain be charged with premeditated murder.[14]

History does not paint a flattering portrait of Andrew R. Wetmore. Jeremiah Travis, a fellow lawyer and a notoriously outspoken contemporary, described him as "grossly and shamelessly dishonest." Travis was amazed Wetmore was ever named attorney general, given his propensity to use language "that could disgrace a brothel." When Wetmore was later made a Supreme Court justice, Travis declared him "the worst judge that has ever disgraced the Bench of our Province."[15]

Wetmore's spicy rhetoric and brazen dishonesty, however, were not what drove him to arrest Cain: it was his obsession with social status. Wetmore had heard the rumours about John Munroe, but he regarded Munroe as an equal, a patrician incapable of wrongdoing.[16] Cain, on the other hand, was a working-class liquor merchant who could not keep his pants fastened, which was more than enough to earn Cain a night in the dungeon.

ELEVEN

Full Cooperation

On Tuesday morning, John Munroe and his lawyer walked into the coroner's office. With quiet dignity, Munroe surrendered himself for what he hoped would be a brief conversation followed by a handshake and an apology from Earle for the nuisance caused. Instead, Munroe and Thomson were forced to wait several hours before the coroner returned from Black River Road.[1] When Earle was finally ready to begin, he politely asked Thomson to remain in the hall during the interview. As a hedge against impropriety, the coroner noted in his records that Munroe "made a statement...voluntarily, without any inducement," adding, "he was a free man at the time."[2]

Munroe entered Earle's office, taking his seat without a trace of apprehension.[3] He launched straight into his account, acknowledging that he knew Maggie Vail, although lately she had taken to calling herself Mrs. Clarke. He mentioned "she had a child," but he could "not say who the child belonged to."[4] Munroe then recounted a conversation he had with Maggie regarding the future of the family home in Carleton. He claimed she wanted to sell the property because of "discord among the family,"[5] a move he strongly advised against, but Maggie had indeed sold the house and moved to Boston, he said, and that was all he knew on the subject.

When Earle asked why Maggie moved to Boston, Munroe recalled the business trip he made to that city one year earlier. He told Earle he'd visited Maggie at her boarding house the day before he left and had mentioned his upcoming journey in passing. Maggie begged him to take her along, but he told her no. He was a married man, after all, and travelling with colleagues; it would have been most improper for her to accompany him. She pleaded, saying she needed "to meet a man there who was going to marry her."[6] Munroe shared what little he knew of Maggie's intended. The man was originally from Saint John but had secured a year's work in Boston. He was a house painter who planned to set down roots with the woman he knew as Mrs. Clarke.[7]

In a casual aside, Munroe confided that Maggie's incessant whining eventually wore him down, so he agreed to take her to Boston. As for the voyage itself, Munroe claimed it passed without incident, for he had little on-board contact with Maggie Vail. He did not see her while in Boston but, entirely by coincidence, shared the same steamer with her on his return. When the boat docked in Saint John, Maggie asked for another favour. She wanted an escort to Loch Lomond, where she would again meet up with her fiancé. From there, she and her painter would travel to Boston to begin their new life together. Although the request made him uncomfortable, Munroe agreed to take Maggie and her daughter out to Black River Road.

When the time came, Munroe said Maggie "wanted him to take her out in a wagon but he did not wish to be seen in her company, and therefore he took her out in a coach." Munroe told Earle that Maggie's destination was a house owned by the Collins family. By then, Earle knew the area well, but he asked Munroe to confirm the location of the house on a map as an added precaution. Recalling one of Robert Worden's statements, the coroner asked Munroe why he ordered the coach to stop so far from the Collins home, obligating the lady to walk an unnecessary distance with a babe in arms. Munroe explained that he feared Maggie's betrothed might see her in his company "and he might not like it."[8]

When they dismounted the carriage, Maggie admitted she was not certain her fiancé had arrived at the Collins house, so she asked Munroe to wait for her while she checked. He took a seat on some large flat rocks as she walked toward the house with Ella on her hip. He later learned they were the same rocks that ultimately became her gravesite. By his reckoning, Munroe waited for almost an hour before Maggie returned, claiming no one was at home at the Collins place. Maggie carried Ella as they walked to Bunker's Tavern, where they met their waiting coachman and returned to Saint John. Munroe added that they left Bunker's with "the understanding...they should go out again."[9]

Thus far the coroner was satisfied with Munroe's account. He would send one of his investigators to question the Collins family as to their whereabouts on the day. He would also have the man time how long it took to walk between the relevant landmarks along the road. The coroner felt certain Munroe's chronology corresponded with the time frame given by Worden.

At Earle's urging, Munroe detailed his second visit to Black River Road. Maggie and Ella once again walked to the Collins house, he said, while he returned to his perch atop the rock. Munroe remembered it had rained off and on in the preceding hours; the ground was wet, and a light drizzle continued to fall. He sat on the rock for almost thirty minutes before Maggie returned with Ella in tow. She told him the Collins family was at home (presumably with her husband-to-be) and that she would stay with them for the remainder of the weekend.

Maggie asked John to retrieve her trunk from the boarding house and have it sent to the docks, as she and her beau were planning to catch the earliest boat to Boston on Monday morning — Mr. Collins generously offered to drive them to the harbour in his carriage — and she would not have time to collect her luggage before they set sail. Munroe agreed to tend to her baggage, and the pair parted ways: Maggie returning to the Collins house and Munroe heading for Bunker's Tavern, where the coach awaited him.

True to his word, Munroe asked Worden to have Mrs. Clarke's trunk transported to the dock, a fact the coachman had already confirmed. Munroe added a final codicil, telling the coroner he had seen Maggie on the dock two days later before her ship sailed for Boston. He travelled to the dock at dawn to ensure her valise had arrived per his instructions. As he made his way through the crowded ship's deck, Munroe said he spotted Maggie just as the final whistle sounded. He rushed to her, pressing the claim tickets for her bags into her hands. Munroe claimed "he only just had time to shake hands with her"[10] before the gangplank lifted and the ship set sail.

Munroe assured Earle that Maggie was alive and well and living in Boston — he'd put her on the departing boat himself. And, the architect reasoned, if Maggie was in Boston, she could not possibly have been lying dead out on Black River Road with her infant daughter at her side. Earle would later recall[11] that nothing in Munroe's statement to that point raised any red flags, but the witness was not finished talking. He felt compelled to add two snippets of information to his statement, data sure to quell whatever lingering doubts the coroner may have. The first was that Miss Vail had recently been spotted about town. Munroe knew a publican, Abram Craft, who would swear he had seen Maggie in his Saint John tavern just five weeks prior. Earle made a note to run down the lead. The second was that Maggie had written letters to her friends and family. Munroe claimed to have received one himself only a month or two previous. When asked if he still had the missive, Munroe regretfully said no; he recalled having thrown it in the trash. Maggie was illiterate, he said, and the spelling in the note was atrocious. Fortunately, Munroe knew of another letter sent to Maggie's sister Philly. Get hold of that letter, Munroe told Earle, and the entire ugly affair could be put to rest.

As the interview drew to a close, Earle gave Munroe a friendly piece of advice. He counselled him to send word to Maggie and ask her to contact the authorities in Boston immediately. The suggestion met with silence as Munroe mulled his options. It was the first inkling Earle had that Munroe knew more than he was telling. Munroe quickly regrouped, saying his lawyer had already advised him not to contact Miss Vail.[12] The statement gave Earle pause. The coroner knew the subpoena issued for Munroe contained no mention of Sarah Margaret Vail. He also knew Thomson had been banished to the hall for the duration of the interview. Munroe's comment implied he and his lawyer had a lengthy conversation about Maggie before Munroe arrived at the coroner's office. Earle thought Munroe's casual aside meant one of two things: either Munroe was lying about Thomson's advice, or he knew full well why he was summoned.

A curious but telling exchange marked the end of the interview. Munroe accurately sensed Earle's growing suspicions, and he lamented that "things looked very black against him."[13] He asked Earle if he was to be arrested. The coroner gave the matter some thought. Earle later told reporters he was not certain he had the authority to arrest Munroe and wanted to consult with the attorney general.[14] When Munroe pressed him again, Earle stated the architect should expect to be taken in before nightfall. Munroe made one last plea to the coroner, a gentlemen's agreement of sorts. He asked for the opportunity to put his affairs in order, begging Earle not to issue a warrant for his arrest. Instead, Munroe swore he would surrender himself to the authorities that night at six o'clock.[15] Such an arrangement ensured him the greatest possible discretion. Earle did not consider Munroe a flight risk, so the two men shook hands to the deal.

John A. Munroe had received his handshake but no apology. He left the coroner's office with his lawyer in tow. He was still a free man, at least for the next few hours.

TWELVE

Hampering and Tampering

Six bells chimed on Tuesday, September 21, 1869, as John Munroe hurried along Prince William Street, the main artery feeding the heart of Saint John. At his side were his younger brother George; Robert Bustin, a maternal relative; and William Roop, Munroe's best friend. The four men were on a mission, though Munroe alone knew its true purpose.

The men soon found themselves on the threshold of No. 118, a tavern of tarnished reputation. John Munroe was a regular patron, well known to its publican, Abram W. Craft. In better days the architect considered No. 118 to be his sanctum sanctorum, a respite from the prying eyes of the world. Those days were now gone, and so the men did what men do in such circumstances: they drank.[1] Although he maintained a facade of cool indifference, John Munroe's brain burned.[2] The time to surrender to authorities had come and gone, making Munroe a fugitive from justice. He retreated to his sanctuary with his most trusted lieutenants to consider his rapidly diminishing options.

His choice of watering hole was no accident. Some five weeks prior, Munroe was seated in the same taproom exchanging confidences with its personable owner. Craft mentioned in passing that the other day a lady stopped by, inquiring after Munroe. When Munroe asked who she was, Craft said it was Miss Margaret Vail of Carleton, and she was most anxious to speak with him. Craft spoke in jest — he'd seen Maggie on the arm of Munroe (whom Craft knew to be a married man) on numerous occasions — and he was looking to rile his philandering customer with some gentle ribbing.[3] Munroe quickly changed the subject as the publican chuckled at his expense.

The night's mission was at last revealed: John Munroe had brought his companions to the tavern to serve as witnesses. At the time, the story of Maggie's visit to No. 118 had annoyed Munroe, but he now needed Craft to repeat the tale within earshot of others. The more people who could attest to the story, the better. After the party took its seats, Munroe called to the publican, asking him to join the table. Before Craft could greet his newest customers, Munroe demanded he recount the specifics of Maggie Vail's recent inquiries. Munroe was visibly distraught as Craft sheepishly confessed to the ruse. An awkward silence descended.

It was now Munroe's turn to confess. He told his compatriots of his impending arrest.[4] Craft knew Munroe only in passing, never having encountered him outside the confines of the barroom. Still, he harboured some guilt for his prior taunt, so he proposed a plan to set things right. Many of Maggie's neighbours were regulars in Craft's establishment. He offered to go to Carleton to inquire as to her current whereabouts. The scheme seemed plausible, and within minutes, Abram Craft sped off toward Carleton in search of Maggie.[5] The quest, however, proved fruitless. Despite repeated inquiries, he could not find anyone who'd seen her in months. A dejected Craft returned to his public house to deliver the news. The trip to Carleton took longer than originally planned, and Craft arrived to discover he was already too late.

Munroe's failure to surrender as promised triggered a series of meetings that culminated in the issuance of an arrest warrant. Just before eight o'clock that evening, Captain Francis Jones "was ordered by the coroner, Attorney General and the Chief of Police to go and get John Munroe."[6] It took only minutes to find the fugitive perched on a barstool at No. 118. Munroe went quietly. No one felt handcuffs were necessary.

At noon on Wednesday, September 22, the usual lunchtime crowds congregated in front of the carts and stalls lining Water Street. The only topic of conversation was the coroner's inquest, which was slated to resume that afternoon. The press had finally learned that Dr. Earle had not one but two suspects in custody, and the morning's papers were filled with speculation. The once-quotidian inquest was now the only thing the public wanted to see. Lines of anxious spectators already stretched for blocks in front of the courthouse doors, which were not scheduled to open for another two hours. Reporters rubbed shoulders with the morbidly curious as everyone jostled to ensure a place in the limited seating.

Lunch was the furthest thing from Earle's mind. The coroner still had too many suspects and no definitive victims. He could not hold the right man accountable until he determined whose bones lay mouldering in the dead house.

The coroner's own bias was also getting in the way. He was certain James Cain was a dyed-in-the-wool adulterer, yet he blithely accepted Munroe's assurances that his relationship with Maggie Vail was purely platonic. Earle was not alone in his assessment. There were tangible differences in the way the police (and the media) treated each suspect. It came down to social class, leaving little doubt whose side the authorities were on: "Mr. Munroe spent last night under the guardianship of the Chief of Police. The man Cain is still detained in jail, and he appears to be quite unconcerned as to the result affecting him one way or another."[7]

The disparity did not stop at creature comforts. The consensus was that Cain was guilty while Munroe was merely the unfortunate victim of a misunderstanding. The *Daily Morning News* noted: "The first of suspicion having lighted on Mr. Munroe (Architect) created a painful sensation throughout the City and fell like a thunderbolt on his many friends. The idea of his being guilty of such a crime, or of anything approaching to crime, seemed to be utterly repudiated as unworthy of belief."[8]

The courthouse doors opened as advertised at two o'clock, and the crowd swarmed in. All pretence of decorum was abandoned when Munroe and Cain were brought into court together. Bustles were rent and toes were trodden as every neck craned to catch a glimpse of Saint John's most notorious duo.[9]

The inequity of the prisoners' respective social stations could not have been more obvious. Munroe, unshackled and dressed to impress, was directed to his table by his equally formidable solicitor. The architect radiated indifference. Cain arrived looking every inch the dangerous criminal, his hands bound, his gait shuffling.[10] Unrepresented by counsel, he was thrust into a chair by the attending constables.[11]

The courthouse was a stone's throw from Munroe's Charlotte Street duplex. The lawful Mrs. Munroe needed only to walk diagonally across King's Square to reach it, if she were so inclined. She was not. She did not make the trip that day or at any other point during the proceedings. If her husband was troubled by his wife's conspicuous absence, he gave no outward indications of distress.

While the two men awaited the arrival of Sylvester Earle, Munroe chatted amiably with the press. One report stated he was "confident that he will come out of this ordeal, for which fortuitous circumstances have subjected him, unscathed." His confidence proved infectious; the *Daily Morning News* brazenly proclaimed "further developments will show"[12] the victims were in fact Cain's mistress and bastard child.

Inquest rules prohibited either man from testifying on his own behalf, so both were forced to sit silently as others determined their fates. Munroe rested comfortably, confident that those speaking on his behalf would sing his praises. Chief among them was Munroe's father, who entered the courtroom "bowed down with a weight of sorrow and grief inexpressible."[13] John Sr. was not called to take the stand. Instead, he took a seat beside a group of reporters, delivering a running commentary throughout the proceedings. In a harsh whisper he alternated between spasms of outrage and ceaseless pleading in an effort to clear his son's name. Following Munroe's arrest, his father had also made a desperate dash to Carleton, but, like Craft, he could not find a single soul who had seen Maggie in the past year. John Sr. vowed to fight on, never resting until his son once again walked free.

First to the stand was the coachman Robert Worden, who spoke of Munroe's multiple forays to Black River Road and of his solo return on Halloween last.[14] Mary Ann Lordly, keeper of the Brunswick House, followed Worden. She recounted Munroe's numerous visits to the "Widow Clarke"[15] and her baby girl who, the landlady noted, bore a striking resemblance to John Munroe.

Lordly also had an eye for fashion, describing specific details of Maggie's clothes. Her astonishing recall gave Earle an idea. He ordered the bailiff to retrieve the scraps of clothing recovered at the crime scene and to present the pieces to the witness. They were vile to the touch and smelt like animal hides, yet Lordly recognized them instantly. In particular, she clearly recalled seeing and complimenting the embroidery work on the hem of Maggie's white skirt, a pignose pattern that was all the rage. She held a scrap of skirt aloft so all could appreciate the stitching. The matted braid of hair was next brought to the stand. Lordly confirmed it was "done up in the style in which [Mrs. Clarke] wore it." Such close proximity to death rattled the normally cantankerous landlady. She said to Earle: "I fear to see any more articles, as those shown strike me so forcibly as belonging to her." The coroner allowed her to step down.[16]

Next to the stand was Sarah Jane Collins, the eldest unmarried daughter and "housekeeper" of the oft-mentioned Collins family. She swore under oath that "no woman and child came to our house during the fall of that year." She was quite certain she had no acquaintance with anyone named Clarke or Vail and knew nothing of a painter bound for Boston. Neither she nor any in her family had ever met John Munroe.[17]

Three other women raised their hands to make life difficult for the architect. Cynthia Dykeman, a seamstress who lived near Maggie, confirmed that the dress recovered from the scene was the very one she'd sewn for Vail a few years prior. "I made the sacque," she declared, "and I do not hesitate to say so."[18] Sarah Lake, who ran the Union Hotel in Saint John, recounted the comings and goings of John Munroe and Mrs. Clarke from her establishment in the days before Maggie went missing. She, too, recognized the clothing and hair as belonging to the woman calling herself Mrs. Clarke. Lake was then shown a small berlin sontag, a hooded V-shaped shawl that draped over the shoulders and crossed in the front just below the waist. Lake's eyes welled with tears and her voice caught in her throat as she said, "I recognize it as that worn by the child."[19] Feeling flush with her recent inheritance, Maggie splurged on the pretty little wrap for Ella during their stay at the Union. Lake had no doubt that it was Ella's sontag: Maggie "sewed those strings on it while at my house."[20] For the second time that afternoon, Dr. Earle feared a witness might swoon on the stand. He allowed Sarah Lake to step down and compose herself.

The last woman called to testify — Jane McLaren, Ella's one-time babysitter — identified more scraps of clothing as belonging to the infant. "I used to dress the baby," she said. "That is the baby's dress; she put that dress upon the baby when she was going away. I am sure." The gallery erupted in sobs as McLaren held up a strange piece of cloth with "a little round hard lump in it." It was Ella's homemade truss, the flattened bullet still stitched inside.[21]

An uncomfortable discussion of Maggie's undergarments, held aloft for all to see the hand-embroidered embellishments, followed. Next came the first mention of jewellery since the berry-pickers' testimony the previous week. Jane McLaren was adamant Maggie always wore a black brooch, "a pin she wore on her sacque."[22] McLaren also recalled "a finger ring with a lump on the back." Maggie never once set foot outside her home without that ring since the day John Munroe gave it to her.[23]

Munroe's detractors were not limited to the fairer sex. Dr. M.H. Peters, the attending physician at Ella's birth, confirmed the truss belonged to the child, although he made clear it was not the one he prescribed. He then recalled an encounter with Phileanor Crear three months earlier. Peters had not seen Maggie for some time, so he asked Philly if she had news of her sister. Philly told the doctor she had just returned from Boston, where she'd searched for her sister to no avail. "Mr. Munroe had hid [Maggie] away in Saint John," Philly said, but she would "find her if she is to be found."[24]

William Lake, proprietor of the Union Hotel, was the next to take a turn in the dock. Without hesitation, Lake pointed to Munroe, saying he "had no doubt"[25] he was the man who paid Mrs. Clarke's bill and arranged for the transport of her trunks to the docks. James Olive, Maggie's brother-in-law and handyman, testified to the five hundred dollars she'd sewn into her bodice following the sale of the Vail home in Carleton.[26] The wretched dress found at the scene was again brought into court. Its neckline was examined, but there was no sign of the money.

In total, eight witnesses stood and told their truths that day. Not one mentioned James Cain. Their testimony did not exonerate Cain in the eyes of the press, however. No matter how bleak things looked for John Munroe, the media still thought Cain was the real killer. When Dr. Earle adjourned the day's proceedings, reporters fled from the courthouse on a mission to proclaim Cain's guilt. Comparisons reveal that published accounts of the afternoon session bore little resemblance to the court transcript. It was as if the press collectively ignored the evidence against Munroe, replacing it with an entrenched contempt for James Cain.

THIRTEEN

The Die Is Cast

Sylvester Earle went over John Munroe's statement with a comb so fine it split hairs, homing in on the one readily verifiable feature: Maggie's supposed voyage to Boston. If she and her luggage had boarded a ferry bound for the United States, as Munroe claimed, some record of the journey must exist. The coroner asked the police chief to investigate, and the chief sent a constable to the docks.

Another idea struck Earle, causing him to make a beeline for the nearest telegraph office. He crafted an urgent message to Phileanor Crear, who was then visiting family in Halifax. In language clipped by technology, he summoned Philly back to Saint John to appear as a witness at the inquest. He instructed her to bring any correspondence she had received from Maggie over the past year.[1] If all went well, this case might be solved by the next day's close of business. Earle made his way back to his office to ready himself for another day in court. Not once had James Cain crossed his mind.

Cain remained uppermost in the thoughts of the press, and Friday, September 23, brought a fresh wave of anti-Cain rhetoric. Three days had passed since any inquest witness spoke of Cain, yet the media continued to discuss his culpability at length. Munroe was barely mentioned, and what little was said of him was quite favourable.

Friday's session saw both men return to court: Munroe looking relaxed and refreshed, Cain dishevelled and fearful. John Munroe Sr. also made an appearance, once again trumpeting his son's innocence.[2] Earle was optimistic as he chatted with the press on his way into court. He hinted a resolution was imminent, leading pundits to predict the day would end with Cain in chains and Munroe's complete exoneration.

Phileanor Crear had yet to respond to the coroner's telegram, so Earle called Louisa Ells, widow of William and mother of three, as the day's first witness.[3] After her husband's untimely death, she took up nursing to pay the bills. Ells told the court she loved Maggie, a girl she had known and raised like her own since Maggie's mother's death. Ells kept a small place near the Vail home in Carleton, where she "was in the habit of seeing [Maggie] every day."[4]

Ells had recommended the lead-bullet truss to fix the baby's rupture, and she wiped away silent tears as she identified the truss as unquestionably the device. More tears fell as she gingerly handled Maggie's matted hair braid, taking in the twigs and filth. "It is very dirty looking but looks like her hair," she testified. "That is the way she wore the braid." The coroner asked Ells to examine the clothing, but she failed to recognize any of it. She said that more than a year had passed since she last saw Maggie "by the Asylum, about a week before she left Carleton." She remembered Maggie was in mourning and her dress was black, though she could not recall its specifics.[5]

Ells's memory improved when she recounted the sale of the Vail house. She recalled a specific conversation she had with Jacob Vail, Maggie's uncle, shortly after the sale and Maggie's disappearance. Vail told her "he believed [Maggie] would give Munroe the money she got from her place and he would spend it and she would be left destitute."[6]

The next witness was a hat maker from Carleton by the name of Jane Campbell. The milliner entered the courtroom sporting her latest creation: a feathered monstrosity worn in a bid to secure some free advertising. Its appearance was especially curious given that Campbell's shop catered to a frugal, downmarket clientele.[7] Campbell "knew the Vail girls" but "did not know their given names." She had served Maggie on two occasions. The first was immediately after the death of her father, when Maggie brought in a "white chip straw [hat], to be coloured black and trimmed with black illusion and black flowers. I think there were also some ribbons on it," Campbell said. Campbell refused to touch the hat recovered at the crime scene. Examining it from a distance, she declared: "The ribbon is like what I had in the shop at the time, and I think I have some of it yet, and the crepe and flowers are the same as I had." Earle asked her to describe the second time she met Maggie. Campbell turned to the jury and said, "A Miss Vail came in and asked about my making a baby's turban for her baby, but she said she could get it cheaper at Mr. Leonard's, and did not order it." With nothing more to add, Jane Campbell and her hat exited the courtroom.[8]

The day's final witness was Daniel Hatfield, an express-wagon driver, whom Robert Worden had identified as the coachman who transported Maggie's trunk from the Union Hotel to the Boston-bound ferry. Earle ordered the hack to appear and Hatfield did as commanded, although his dazed and distracted manner suggested he came by way of a tavern.

At times Hatfield could not remember where he was or why. Worse still, his short-term memory exceeded his long-term recall. When asked if he had delivered Maggie's trunk to the dock, the decipherable portions of his testimony read: "I remember *slightly* going to Mr. Lake's for trunks...but I don't remember whether I took it to the American boat or to the [unintelligible]. Don't remember when it was or what time it was. Don't know who paid me nor anything about it."[9] Not surprisingly, there were no follow-up questions, and Daniel Hatfield stumbled out the way he came.

Hatfield's confusion was a boon for Munroe, yet he seemed indifferent. One reporter noted:

> Munroe gave little evidence of the feeling that one would suppose a man in his position should experience. Indeed, we observed quite frequently that he was engaged in apparently agreeable conversation with persons sitting near him, smiling pleasantly and seemingly taking little interest in the tragic business going on in Court.... We noticed this apparent nonchalant manner on his part more than once, even when the most telling testimony was being presented.[10]

Munroe was so certain of his eventual acquittal that the actual mechanics of the inquest were of little interest to him.

Despite the press's prognostications of Cain's impending doom, the day ended with the scales of justice tipped in his favour. After a moment of sober reflection, Sylvester Earle called the grocer forward. Cain stood in expectant silence as Earle drafted an agreement releasing him from custody. The writ required a cash bond as well as the signatures of two sureties, upstanding citizens who would guarantee Cain would again surrender himself before the court should the need arise. The necessary funds and guarantors were eventually found, and the paperwork was executed to the satisfaction of all, save perhaps for Munroe. As unexpectedly as it began, Cain's nightmare ended. His cuffs were removed. He was free to go and sin no more.

ACT THREE

In which the Crown ponders evidence of Munroe's actions and intent, or the court debates his character.

FOURTEEN

"Rumours Both Grave and Ridiculous"

James Cain walked free as Sylvester Earle gavelled the session to a close. The hearing would resume again on Monday afternoon, giving the jury the weekend to tend to domestic matters. After the courtroom cleared, reporters appeared too stunned to bolt. Their confusion did not stem from the abrupt legal about-face, for such sharp reversals made for good copy. No, what vexed the city's newshounds were John Munroe and his lack of emotion. The architect did not look or act like a killer, leaving the press frantically searching for cracks in the man's impeccable facade.

They soon found a fissure. The public character analysis of John Munroe began with some unverifiable allegations — "rumours both grave and ridiculous"[1] — cropping up in the city's broadsheets. One particular story captured the headlines for days, fuelled by its undertones of homoerotic misadventure. It began when the *Daily Morning News* reported that, two nights before the alleged murders, "Mr. Graham, the proprietor of the Fredericton *Head Quarters*," spent the evening with John Munroe in a Woodstock hotel. The two men shared a room containing two beds. Late in the evening, "Munroe exhibited strong signs of perturbation, walking the floor and finally begging to be permitted to get into Mr. Graham's bed, which was granted."[2]

The *News* had been stalwart in its support of Munroe, which made the editor's decision to run the story all the more confounding. To mitigate the report's destructive impact, the paper downplayed its significance, stating the tale was simply "an indication that [Munroe] was troubled with unquiet conscience," and that "such a 'trifle light as air' as this, even though true, does not prove anything against Mr. Munroe."[3]

The paper's chief rival, the *St. John Daily Telegraph and Morning Journal*, was also decidedly pro-Munroe. Its editorial board watched dumbstruck as sales of the *News* skyrocketed thanks to the Graham exclusive. On October 2, the *Telegraph* lured back readers by running a letter from Graham, who categorically denied the incident in Woodstock ever took place. What offended Graham most was not his association with a suspected multiple murderer but the suggestion he'd shared his bed with another man.

Anxious to keep the story alive, the *Daily Morning News* published a telegram from the original source of the story, William Paisley. Paisley worked for the post office, a fact the *News* highlighted as though it conveyed some measure of credibility. Paisley called Graham out, saying the story was told "by Mr. Graham in my presence, and can be proved by several parties who were present when he made such statements."[4] The normally sedate *Fredericton Reporter* waded into the fray when it announced another man had stepped forward to support Paisley's claims.[5] Neither Graham nor Paisley was ever called to give testimony before the coroner or any other authority; the episode in the hotel room was never formally introduced into evidence. The newspaper coverage remains the lone record of the incident, but the story is telling both for what it reveals of Munroe's character and for its insights into prevailing attitudes toward homosexuality.

Other newspaper-borne viruses soon swept through New Brunswick. The *Reporter* ran a troubling story. In May 1868, John Munroe, Maggie Vail, and Ella visited Fredericton and stayed in one of the area's dicier hotels, registered as man and wife. One morning, they went to a saloon for a breakfast of oysters, long-touted as a folk remedy for hangovers. The barkeep, Caribel Allen, told the *Reporter* that Munroe's "strange conduct and indifference to his wife, her rather shabby appearance and the neglected look of the child" appalled him.[6]

A far more incendiary whisper that began in the press soon made its way to the coroner's hearing. The *Daily Morning News* announced, "Miss Vail was some five months advanced in pregnancy at the time of her murder."[7] Rival papers dismissed this shocking allegation as "a statement that is more easily made than proved."[8] In a closed session, the coroner asked Dr. Christie, who performed Maggie's autopsy, whether the report was true. Unfortunately, the decomposed state of her remains precluded a medical confirmation of the rumour. The *News* refused to reveal its source, so the credibility of the claim cannot be assessed. When the issue was raised in open court, Munroe appeared "quite calm, his countenance expressing neither alarm...nor indignant surprise at the web being woven around him."[9]

Whether or not the prospect of a second illegitimate child was Munroe's motive for murder is, now and forever, a question without answer.

John Munroe had spent his first night in custody in relative luxury, bedded down in the den of the chief of police. Following Cain's release, Munroe was given the grocer's vacated cell in the county lock-up. In an ironic footnote, Munroe had been contracted as the lead architect for a series of improvements to the Saint John jail just six months prior.[10] He was already intimately familiar with his cell, having personally overseen its renovation in the past weeks. Had he any inkling of his fate, he might have given more thought to the creature comforts it afforded.

FIFTEEN

A Skull Wrapped in Meat

Although James Christie was a licensed physician, he fancied himself an artist. He often abandoned the scientific method in favour of his intuition, cobbling together his research designs from hunches and an eye for the dramatic. As the pathologist tasked with interpreting the bony remnants of two lives cut short, James sketched loose portraits of the victims from Black River Road: a well-to-do woman in her twenties and an infant of indeterminate sex and age.

Having done what little he could with the question of who, Christie then turned his attention to how. Although the child's cause of death left no discernible trace on the surviving bones, it was obvious the woman was shot in the head. But where was the bullet? The projectile entered the skull, but there was no corresponding exit wound. No slug was recovered from inside the brain cavity, nor was one found amidst the rotting grey matter left behind at the scene. What, the doctor wondered, became of the fatal shot?

Christie decided to experiment. He went to his cabinet of curiosities— standard accoutrement for scientific men of the age—and selected a skull, a cleaned anatomical preparation of unknown provenance. He set the skull on a table in his office, pulled a Smith & Wesson .22 calibre pistol from his desk drawer,[1] and, from a distance of two feet, fired into the left temple. "The bullet went through both sides and mashed the skull a good deal,"[2] Christie later reported. He had inadvertently obliterated a perfectly good teaching specimen.

The doctor was not satisfied. He suspected the fault lay in the execution rather than the research design. The problematic variable was the test subject: a clean dry skull was not a suitable analogy for a fleshed head. Christie hurried about his surgery gathering up the necessary materials, including another cranium. To simulate a fresh human head, he "covered the skull with a muscular tissue and filled the skull nearly full with water." Christie never elaborated as to the source of the "muscular tissue" or specified how he kept the water inside a sectioned skull.[3]

Christie placed the leaking, meat-wrapped bundle on the table and took up his pistol. He positioned himself at arm's length from the unholy chimera and fired two shots directly into the skull's left temple. When he then freed the skull from its fleshy coverings, he discovered "neither of them went through — both bullets dropped through into the skull." Christie declared the experiment a smashing success.[4]

No professional guidelines governed Christie's experiments, save for common sense. Ethical concerns aside, there was the very real possibility of harming his wife (who was seated in the next room), not to mention the fear multiple gunshots might invoke in his neighbours. To Christie's way of thinking, however, these possibilities were a small price to pay to prove his theory and advance scientific knowledge.

It was all for naught. The experiment's results did not tangibly contribute to the investigation, for nothing was learned that was not already known. Both Christie and Botsford had already estimated the calibre of weapon from the dimensions of the wound.[5] The wound track indicated the bullet entered the skull but did not exit, and his test did nothing to help find the missing projectile. Indeed, the only question the test answered was one never raised: had the skull been shot long after death as it lay, bare and desiccated, on the forest floor?[6] For all the moral affronts the experiment offered, the doctor was no closer to solving the mystery than before he opened fire.

In a curious aside, Christie's questionable methods raised no hue or cry among his learned colleagues, though he did catch flak from the public. During his initial appearance at the coroner's inquest on September 30 — Christie's first public disclosure of his experiments — he recounted the tests conducted on "the skull,"[7] implying he'd used the actual remains from the crime scene. The slip caused many observers to question the doctor's decision to repeatedly shoot a dead woman in the head, particularly after draping the skull in meat of unknown origin.

When Dr. Christie was recalled during the trial, he made a crucial semantic shift. When asked to describe his efforts, he made clear they were conducted "on a skull in the office." This statement was only marginally less disturbing, as it suggested he kept human heads lying about waiting to be shot. Christie distanced himself from his poor choices by insisting, "I did not fire the shot myself in the experiment, it was done under my direction," contradicting his prior inquest testimony.[8]

Still, Christie's lapses in judgment ignited a frenzy of experimentation that bore little resemblance to reliable scientific investigation. The next efforts came from the media. John March, who was "connected with the *Daily Morning News*,"[9] and David G. Smith, "a reporter on the *Telegraph* newspaper,"[10] decided to visit the crime scene. They were unable to find it initially. In desperation they enlisted the help of local publican Horace Bunker, who led them to the shallow depression between two large rocks where the bodies were found. Everything about the location invited malice, for no place on earth seemed more amenable to disposing of a murdered mother and child. The gap between the rocks formed a ready-made grave, particularly when covered with brush cut from the nearby trees. Moreover, the spot was isolated.

The reporters decided to see just how isolated. While March stood atop the larger rock, Smith paced back to the road.[11] The two reporters lost sight of one another almost immediately. Smith repeatedly called out as he walked along the path to the roadway. When the trail bent sharply at 150 feet, Smith shouted, "I see you!" He continued to the road, reaching it just as a horse and carriage passed by. He could no longer see March on the rock, although March later claimed that, when he stood on the very tips of his toes, he "could see the top of the wagon there and the people but couldn't see the horses; and then only saw them for an instant."[12]

When asked what they hoped to accomplish, March told authorities he'd "made the observations for the purposes of my paper." The reporters' brief foray into the world of crime scene investigation led them to draw a number of conclusions. The first was that the sightlines from the road to the burial site were often unobstructed. March testified: "If a female were standing upon the rock, a person driving could see her, I think."[13] Smith concurred, adding that a passing carriage driver "might possibly see a man and woman on the rock at any season."[14]

David Smith also expounded on the quality of the soil, specifically its effect on the rate of decomposition. "The nature of the ground is such that in winter a body might be there some time without decaying," he testified. "I do not think it would be less able to decay in the summer."[15] In 1869 the rules of evidence were so lenient that such inexpert conjecture was admitted into the inquest record without challenge. Equally shameful was that the press thought to conduct such experiments, yet the idea never occurred to law enforcement.

The urge to experiment at the crime scene proved contagious. Four interested bystanders — David Carroll, David Heffernon, Charles A. Raymond, and Adam Young — conducted trials of their own. David Carroll, a plumber by trade, carried with him a Smith & Wesson .22, the gun of choice for murderers and armchair sleuths alike. Carroll stood on the same large rock and "sent some of the party toward [the road] to ascertain how far the shots would be heard."[16] All clearly heard his first two shots. Carroll followed with five more rounds as the men moved farther afield. Each time, they had no trouble hearing the gun's report.[17] The men established two facts beyond all reasonable doubt: one, while the sightlines from the road to the grave were sometimes obscured, the sound of gunshots travelled unhindered; and two, those without badges or investigative training once again bested the police.

The test may have been unbiased, but these amateur sleuths were not. At least three of them had a personal relationship with John Munroe. "As a plumber," Carroll said, "I had frequent intercourse with him as an architect."[18] Adam Young claimed to "have known [Munroe] some time almost intimately."[19] David Heffernon was a liquor merchant who lived a few doors down from Munroe on Charlotte Street.[20] Charles Raymond's connection to Munroe is difficult to discern, as he was never called to testify and has left little trace in the historical record. On the stand, Carroll and Young sang Munroe's praises in remarkably similar keys. Said Young: "His disposition was quiet, amiable and kind — particularly so. I should not think him a person capable of committing such a crime. He is almost the last person I would have suspected."[21] Carroll echoed the sentiment, adding, "I always thought him a quiet, inoffensive man.... He generally had little to say when I went to him on business. I never saw anything in his conduct to induce me to suppose him capable of committing such a crime."[22]

Phileanor Crear received the coroner's summons in the final week of September and immediately boarded a steamer ship bound for Saint John. So great was the anticipation of her testimony, the *Daily Morning News* printed her travel itinerary with the treatment normally reserved for the royal family.[23] The trip from Halifax to Saint John is two hundred kilometres as the crow flies, but the voyage took two days, giving the press ample time to speculate. One widely reported rumour claimed Philly carried a letter that would completely exonerate John Munroe.

Philly, however, was determined to see Munroe hanged for his crimes and took every opportunity to impugn him. In press interviews Philly said her sister idolized Munroe, despite repeated warnings from friends and family. Maggie's infatuation was so intense, Philly said, she would have "nothing to do with any other man." According to Philly, that blind devotion cost her dearly.[24]

On the morning of Thursday, September 30, Philly claimed her seat in the dock. Raising her hand to God, she proceeded to wreak havoc on John Munroe's character. In testimony spanning more than five hours, the inquest's star witness began by sketching the Vail family tree, noting, "There are six sisters of us; there is one dead and I expect another is." She recalled Ella's birth, erasing any lingering doubts as to the child's paternity: "I know it because no other man kept company with [Maggie] from the first to the last, and she told me [Ella] was his." She described the child's hernia, along with the fashioning of the truss. When shown the recovered bandage, Phileanor declared, "If I should be struck dead this minute, that is the lead bullet.... I could swear to it if I was on my death bed." She also identified other scraps of clothing, in particular a section of a tiny dress: "So help me God, this is the stuff."[25]

Philly was holding up well. She seemed more angry than sad, with an especially determined set to her jaw. Dr. Earle asked her to describe the child's overall appearance. She started with Ella's hair, noting it "was white —it could not be any whiter; it was short and glistening." The bailiff opened a small box, removing a tangle of hair that he placed before the witness. Philly stared at the knotted mass, pausing to wipe away a single tear before stating: "This could not be more like it, but it is soiled by laying out." She bristled at Earle's follow-up question, in which he asked her to gauge the certainty of her recollections. "It would not be any easy thing for me to be deceived in the hair," Philly snorted, "for I had the washing and dressing of the baby to do."[26]

The identification process turned to the adult remains. One by one, the tattered scraps of clothing were paraded before the witness. Phileanor's conviction grew stronger with every article. She peppered her testimony with exacting detail, recounting where and when each piece was purchased. She handled each exhibit without recoiling, as if its meaning could be derived through touch, like Braille. As the morning wore on and the sheriff neared the end of his exhibits, a thick section of black ribbon was presented. For whatever reason, Philly finally cracked, her strength exhausted. "That is her waist ribbon," she whispered, "I bought it in James Manson's [shop]."[27] In the court transcript, the clerk's notation reads: "The witness broke down and began to weep bitterly."[28] The coroner adjourned the session for lunch.

The hearing resumed just after two o'clock. Phileanor was dry-eyed and calm, revealing no trace of her prior dismay. The bailiff approached with a matted braid of thick brown hair. It was clear to all she recognized the hair, and with it came the brutal certainty Maggie was dead. "Oh, it is too true — my poor, poor sister; she is gone!" Philly wailed. "This is more than I can stand... Oh, to have to look at my poor sister's hair that has been so cruelly murdered...Oh, how could he be so cruel as to do it!...Oh, poor Mag, you're gone—you're gone! And to think that she should lie in the snow all winter!"[29]

A final exhibit was drawn from its box: the adult skull aerated with its fatal bullet wound. In a cringe-worthy nod to Shakespeare's poor Yorick, Phileanor held the skull in her hand and stared into its vacant eye sockets as she delivered a maudlin soliloquy to her murdered kin: "Oh, is that the way I have to look at you now, when I used to be able to look at your features and now can see nothing but your poor skeleton!" She dried her eyes as the skull was carried from the courtroom.[30]

Earle redirected Philly's attention to the issue of Maggie's inheritance. Like Maggie's uncle and neighbour before her, Phileanor swore under oath that Munroe coerced Maggie into giving him the five hundred dollars from the sale of the house, although no one could offer any proof to substantiate their claims. Munroe's father had already denied the allegations to reporters, arguing his son's prodigious wealth made such larceny unnecessary. In the end, all Philly could say with any certainty was that Maggie's bosom was the last known location of the money, and the only man with the key to that treasure chest was John A. Munroe.[31]

Earle asked if Phileanor might recognize her sister's lover if she saw him again. Her contempt was palpable as she spat out her reply: "I should know John Munroe if I saw him. I have had my eye on him once or twice in court, and I should not like to be very near him or see him again."[32] The outburst had no visible effect on Munroe or his defence lawyer. Phileanor served only one purpose for the prisoner: to deliver the exculpatory letter. On that score, she did not disappoint.

At Earle's urging, Phileanor produced the letter, a single page written in a self-consciously childish hand, still nestled in its original envelope and bearing all the stamps and postmarks necessary to recall its journey. She told the court how and when she received it before trying to hand it to the clerk. Earle asked her to read it into evidence. Blushing, Philly said she was illiterate and asked if someone else might read it aloud. The clerk complied, doing his best to convey the note's numerous spelling and grammatical errors. Philly was quick to add her sister was also illiterate and could not possibly have written the note. She was now certain the letter was "in Mr. Munroe's handwriting." She chased the accusation with a heated glance at the defence table. Philly claimed she always knew the note's author. "The letter came from Mr. Munroe to deceive me if he could." The second she received it, she knew "he had done away with the girl — made away with her for the sake of her money, and to get her off his hands." In a quieter voice, she admitted she had not shared her suspicions with anyone at the time.[33]

Having reached its crescendo, Philly's testimony was suspended. It would not be her only appearance at the inquest, but it would be hard to top this performance for sheer bravado. As for what legal impact it might have, only time would tell.

In spite of Philly Crear's impassioned testimony, many still doubted John Munroe had written the letter. It was too melodramatic a turn for such a pragmatic and educated man. Those who were convinced Munroe was its author saw it as an audaciously calculated move. Neutral observers were left to marvel at the ingenuity of the scheme, and at the purity of its failure.

The letter was too compelling for the press to ignore. After Phileanor stepped down from the dock, the *Daily Morning News* belied its name by rushing a special late-afternoon edition onto the streets. The handbill contained full coverage of her explosive turn on the witness stand, including a verbatim reprint of the letter. The paper also tried something scandalously new: it enlisted the services of a graphologist, a self-proclaimed expert in handwriting analysis. Although the use of such experts is now commonplace in cable news programs, this is the earliest known example of the press embracing this particular brand of infotainment.

Readers were left to speculate as to the training of the so-called expert, but what he lacked in credentials, he made up in verbosity. His front-page diatribe exceeded the length of the letter by a factor of a hundred. The report contained numerous insights into the character and vocation of the letter's author. The letter *g* was scripted in "the style of business men,"[34] and the formation of the letter *p* in the word "painter" revealed the repressed anger of the writer. The syntax and purposeful spelling mistakes, he argued, indicated a desire to deceive. At no point did the expert (or indeed the authorities) compare the letter to any known sample of Munroe's handwriting.

The news feature was no doubt intended to be cutting edge, though it now reads as a quaint artifact. The analysis neither inculpated nor exonerated Munroe. Indeed, it contributed nothing to the ongoing debate. The graphology examination was riddled with gross generalizations and unfounded pseudoscientific observations. In short, it bore all the hallmarks of Victorian reportage: it was new, but it was not news.

SIXTEEN

Photo Finish

On October 1, 1869, Captain H.W. Chisholm reported for duty as usual. Despite his rank and his ramrod posture, Chisholm had no military affiliation. He was a booking agent for the International Steamship Company, presently stationed in Saint John Harbour. He began his workday with a review of the morning's post, which included a letter from W.H. Kilby, Chisholm's counterpart in the company's Boston affiliate. Each agent was responsible for the passenger and cargo manifest of the steamer *New York*, which regularly plied the Bay of Fundy's waters. The letter, sent September 27, read:

> *Dear Sir* – Last week I had a despatch and letter from the Chief of Police, at St. John, asking if we had here a black trunk and valise marked "Mrs. Clark" or "Sarah M. Vail." We overhauled our stock of unclaimed baggage without finding any such marks. This morning, Mr. Fletcher was reading in the *Daily Telegraph* the testimony of Sarah Lake, in which she states there were two trunks, one inside the other, and he remembered [seeing] such a truck.... [W]e have made another examination and have found the baggage.... There is a parasol and a few articles of woman's and child's clothing which don't look very neat.... Please notify the authorities. I will send it by the *New York* Thursday.
>
> Yours truly, W.H. Kilby.[1]

Chisholm ran to his office window just as the steamer sailed into view. The trunk was on board as promised, hand-carried by the ship's mate, John S. Hall, who never let it out of his sight.[2] Chisholm sent a runner to notify the coroner and police chief their evidence had arrived.

The authorities already knew, having received their own cable from Kilby two days prior. So did the press, as well as anyone in possession of the morning's broadsheets. An unruly crowd was gathering in the square outside the courthouse, anxious for the first glimpse of the newly uncovered baggage. Those closest to the courthouse steps stood with their eyes focused on the locked doors.

At precisely ten o'clock on the morning of Saturday, October 2, those doors flung open, and pandemonium ensued. Men muscled women aside for a coveted seat in the gallery, while the truly determined scaled the barricades.[3] That such a rumpus was to see a piece of unclaimed baggage made the spectacle all the more bewildering. Less than two minutes after the doors opened, an eerie calm descended over the courtroom. The only sounds were the reproachful calls of the bailiffs ordering spectators to climb down from the jury box. The louts reluctantly complied, only to be escorted from the courthouse with a stern lecture on the need for solemnity.

The crowd's fevered efforts were soon rewarded. Those in the gallery stared as the court clerks carried in the day's main attraction: "Mrs. Clarke's trunk." Its reverential reception was at odds with its humble appearance. Covered in black oilcloth topped with three wooden straps, the case looked as if it had "received tough usage in travelling, but showed little signs of wear."[4]

The trunk so engrossed the crowd that few noticed as the jury took their seats. The inquest was set to resume. The coroner ascended the bench, calling for his witness. Captain Chisholm took his seat in the dock. The captain's regal bearing and stentorian tone marked him as a man in the know. At the coroner's behest, Chisholm read aloud from the letter he received outlining the trunk's journey from the company's unclaimed storage locker in Boston to where it sat in the courtroom. It then fell to Chisholm to preside over the hearing's most anticipated moment. A faint tremor shook his otherwise steady hand as he unclasped the lock and opened the trunk.

Spectators hoping for a dead body or the murder weapon were sorely disappointed, for the chest's musty confines held no gore or ill omen. Over the next hour, an exhaustive inventory of the trunk's contents was made as Chisholm held up and described each item in turn. The valise was a portable museum of the failed romantic. Its pink- and white-striped interior held a collection of mundane items: clothing for a woman and an infant, sewing notions, a parasol, many newspapers and other printed materials, a few loose candies, and a badly decayed apple.[5]

Just as all hope of a smoking gun seemed lost, a small parcel wrapped in newspaper emerged. Chisholm laid the bundle upon the prosecutor's table and carefully released its binding. Inside was a series of photographs, including a tintype of a man, encased in a decorative frame. The photo, Chisholm said, bore an unmistakable likeness to the prisoner. He held the photo overhead as the crowd erupted in frantic whispers. No one could deny it was John Munroe. There was now irrefutable proof linking the architect to the elusive Mrs. Clarke.

The coroner pounded his gavel until his arm ached, drawing the room to some semblance of order. Five more witnesses were called to the stand, each claiming to have seen the trunk in Mrs. Clarke's possession in the days before she disappeared.[6] To put all doubt to rest, Mrs. Phileanor Jane Crear made her second appearance in as many days. She went item by item through the trunk. A locket of hair evoked the strongest reaction. "This is my poor father's hair," said Philly, "I cut it off his temple with my own hands, and divided it with my sister."[7]

The final item examined was the packet of photographs. Philly did not hesitate to put a name to each face. "This is my oldest brother, Jacob Vail, who is now in Minnesota," she said. "That is my own [face]; this is aunt Margaret Nickerson and her husband, who is in Canada."[8] Finally, the bailiff handed Philly the framed tintype. She refused to handle it, saying, "It is hardly necessary to ask who that is: it is John Munroe, the murderer who ruined my sister and then murdered her; how could he do so." Earle cut the tirade off midstream, asking Philly how Maggie obtained the image. "I am positive he brought it," Philly replied, "for I asked him for one at the same time, and he promised to give me one. That is the same photograph. She had no other." Philly savoured the moment, for there was a certain irony in the fact that a by-product of John Munroe's vanity could be his undoing.[9]

The inquest's final witness was Captain Francis S. Jones of the Portland police. The lawman cut a fine figure, as sharp as the snip of a tailor's scissors. He was fond of his uniform and wore it well, enjoying the respect its dark blue serge aroused in others. Jones was in the twenty-second year of his thirty-year reign as Portland's first police chief. He held the post from his appointment in 1847 to his retirement in 1877, minus the few years he stepped aside due to poor health.[10]

Jones took the Bible in hand, swearing to be truthful. Since inquest rules prohibited Sylvester Earle from testifying, Jones was called to do it for him. The chief was privy to most of the coroner's interviews, and Munroe passed his first night in custody on Mrs. Jones's horsehair sofa.

Jones was a stickler for rules. Prior to all official interviews, he made a point of telling his prisoner "he had better be cautious what he said... as [I] might be called on the stand." Munroe took little heed of the warning, according to Jones, stating that "what he would tell us he would tell himself if he was put on the stand."[11]

Munroe told the police the same story he gave the coroner: he barely knew Miss Vail, had no notion as to the child's paternity, and only agreed to take the woman and her child out to Black River Road so she could meet her fiancé. According to Jones, Munroe last saw Maggie on the dock in Saint John when she boarded the steamer to Boston. Beyond that, the accused knew only that she and her baby were keeping house in the States with some painter named Crandall. Although Jones was called to say what the coroner could not, he served as Munroe's mouthpiece as well. The police chief's testimony entered Munroe's statements into the record without exposing the accused to cross-examination, an added benefit from the perspective of Munroe's lawyer.

After Jones vacated the witness stand, the coroner paused to gather his thoughts. He had no more witnesses to call, no more evidence to dissect. The hearing had lasted nearly three weeks, presenting the sometimes poignant, sometimes pointless, testimony of fifty-two witnesses.[12] All that remained was for Earle to instruct the jury so it might render a verdict.

He opened his address to the jury with an admission of his own failings. "This was all the evidence he had to offer," but "if it was necessary he would read it to them" again. The jury politely declined his offer. The coroner asked the jury to answer three questions: "Who the parties were whose remains were found; if they came to their death by foul means; and if so, by whose hand the deed was done." He then released the panel to begin their deliberations.[13]

The seven-man jury retired at five o'clock, asking only for the transcript of evidence and a copy of Philly's letter. Those seated in the gallery had a choice to make: await the verdict or vacate their seats, mindful that every empty chair would be snapped up one of the hangers-on stationed outside the courthouse. Every spectator held his ground.

They would not wait long. The panel returned with its verdict less than forty-five minutes later. Foreman John Daly stood and, with trembling hands and voice, declared: "The remains found were those of Sarah Margaret Vail, and she came to her death by a pistol shot fired by the hand of John A. Munroe, on the 31st day of October, 1868." Earle's gavel silenced the murmurs eddying through the court, and Daly read from the second writ, which "also found a verdict of Wilful Murder against John A. Munroe for the murder of Ella May Munroe, infant child of Sarah Margaret Vail."[14]

Stunned reporters leapt from their seats. One local editor wrote: "The Coroner then made out his warrants committing John A. Munroe to the care of the Sheriff for safe keeping till set free by due course of law."[15] Note the wording "till set free" — an implicit understanding that a wrongfully accused Munroe would soon be released.

The *Saint John New Dominion and True Humorist* also cast its lot with Munroe, imploring its readers to withhold judgment until the trial:

> Darkly as the clouds gather over Monroe [*sic*], let him have justice. Let there be no prejudgment, difficult as it may be to resist the inference inevitable from the *prima facie* case.... When this is done society will breathe freer; because an innocent man will be restored to the full enjoyment of the rewards of his till and the advantages of citizenship.[16]

Saint John's warring dailies, the *St. John Daily Telegraph and Morning Journal* and the *Daily Morning News*, also admonished readers to give John Munroe the benefit of the doubt. In so doing, they gave far greater weight to their perceptions of his character than to the circumstantial case against him.

SEVENTEEN

Morbidity and Mortality

In 1869 the Canadian legal system was needlessly convoluted and prone to duplicated effort. Coroner's inquests ended with verdicts but not indictments. The formal laying of charges required another hearing before a police magistrate, followed by a grand jury.[1] At each step the exact same testimony was revisited in full. Throw in the inevitable trial and every case was presented in court no fewer than four times before a final verdict was reached.

As the accused sat in a hell of his own renovation, it fell to police magistrate Humphrey T. Gilbert to determine if the Crown had the evidence to keep him there. Few men were better suited to the task, for Gilbert "was of Loyalist origin and it was easy for him to show his descent from and connection with that eminent Sir Humphrey Gilbert, famed in song and history."[2] Yet another Sir Humphrey T. Gilbert, an eponymous descendant, arrived on New Brunswick's eastern shore in 1783 and soon spawned a legal dynasty. One of his sons, also named Humphrey, was a magistrate in Westmorland County, where Humphrey the third was born and reared. The youngest Humphrey left briefly to study law and was admitted to the bar in 1843, just shy of his thirtieth birthday. In May 1858, H.T. Gilbert was appointed police magistrate of Saint John, a post he would hold for almost twenty-four years.

On Tuesday, October 6, 1869 — the day John A. Munroe was first escorted into his courtroom — Humphrey Gilbert was fifty-five years old. He ruled his bench with a steady hand, resplendent in his robes, fanatically proud of his illustrious ancestry, and ever so slightly intoxicated by his own allure. Gilbert enjoyed presiding over the most contentious, high-profile case in the land. There was no need for a jury, for this was a decision Humphrey must make on his own.

His examination ran for six days, well short of Earle's protracted inquest and "nearly all the witnesses who had testified at the Inquest were examined by the Magistrate."[3] The press largely ignored the proceedings, but two witnesses did capture headlines. The first was Sylvester Earle, free at last to discuss the case at length. Munroe, his lawyer, and a handful of reporters sat in Gilbert's chambers as the coroner recounted his initial tour of the crime scene and cursory examination of the remains. Earle had strong opinions as to when the victims died: "I was convinced that they had lain there from the fall previous. I was led to that conclusion by the state of the brush, the clothing and the bones."[4] It was the first time anyone heard of Earle's uncannily accurate time-since-death estimate, but it would not be the last.

The second witness to awaken the press gaggle was the ever-boisterous Phileanor Crear. Gilbert "urged" his witness "to refrain, if possible, from the exhibition of any feeling against the prisoner." Phileanor made no such promises. She began with a reprise of her inquest statements then segued into a rehash of the night Munroe asked Maggie to poison his wife. Less than one year later, her flippant prediction that she would one day repeat his question in court had come true. She shook her head in disbelief. "I said it in fun," she told Gilbert, "not thinking it would ever come to this or that I should be called on to do it."[5]

Philly expanded on the tale. One week after Munroe first suggested killing his wife, he reappeared at the Vail home. He once again brazenly asked Maggie if she would poison his wife. Philly overheard the conversation, but this time she sensed the architect was not speaking in jest. She told the judge she had shown Munroe the door and ordered him never to return.

Munroe's lawyer strongly objected to her testimony. He demanded to know why she never mentioned the second alleged poisoning plot during her inquest testimony. Philly waved off the question, saying "she had not been asked."[6] The judge overruled the objection. It was now Thomson's turn to shake his head in disbelief. He knew the accusation would come back to haunt his client at trial and that now, thanks to Phileanor and her evidence of premeditation, there would undoubtedly be a trial.

On the sixth day, the witness pool exhausted, Justice Gilbert took a moment of sober deliberation before declaring: "It was clear that a murder had been committed." He rhetorically posed and then answered two questions. "Who had been murdered? He thought the evidence most clear on that point, and even the prisoner himself must acknowledge that it could be no other than Sarah Margaret Vail."[7] Gilbert then asked: "Who committed the deed?" On this count, "every circumstance pointed so strongly to the prisoner that the Magistrate could not do otherwise than commit him for trial."[8]

Despite his conclusions, Gilbert clearly sympathized with the accused. "The magistrate was visibly affected during his remarks to the prisoner," one observer noted. "It caused him sorrow to see [Munroe] in such a position." Even as the judge ordered the sheriff to take the architect into custody, Gilbert assured the court that Munroe "would yet be able to show his innocence" and prayed "that the dark cloud hanging over him might be dispelled." Before the judge gavelled an end to the proceedings, he had one last piece of advice for the architect. Gilbert knew well the dangers of hubris. He looked Munroe square in the eye, imploring him to "remember that he was mortal." Munroe said nothing, his face betraying no emotion as he was remanded into custody.[9]

Thomson hoped to spare his client the indignities of long-term incarceration, but anyone accused of murder was statutorily denied bail. Munroe returned to the city jail, a building years past its prime despite the recent spate of renovations. There were repeated calls to close the facility, but public coffers were low, crime was high, and not everyone remembered they were mortal.

EIGHTEEN

The Obvious Child

Infants are such fragile creatures. They are incapable of fending for themselves and succumb to the faintest whiff of disease. In the 1800s, children died. It was a sad fact of life, but a fact nevertheless. One of the unspoken reasons couples had such large families was that a certain degree of attrition was to be expected.

The delicate nature of the newly born evoked a curious response among the gentler classes—children were not merely sexless but also without gender. In moneyed circles, all infants were dressed as dolls, making it virtually impossible to differentiate boys from girls. Many a Victorian male started life as a tiny transvestite bedecked in the same rococo ruffles as his sisters. This gender-neutral policy extended to the use of pronouns, including the ubiquitous practice of referring to any child as "it." Ella May Munroe was no exception. Not once in the recorded proceedings or newspaper interviews did Munroe call his child by name. On the rare occasion he made any allusion to her, she was simply "it."[1] In fairness to Munroe, Philly also addressed her niece in that manner.

There were other era-specific cultural norms. In Victorian social hierarchy men reigned supreme (Her Majesty being the lone notable exception), followed distantly by women, and then, lagging far behind, children. English law granted men absolute rights over their wives and progeny. Upon marriage, women and offspring became the property of the paterfamilias; as chattel, they could be dealt with as their owner saw fit.[2] The law afforded children few protections. In 1853 the legislature introduced the Act for the Better Prevention and Punishment of Aggravated Assaults upon Women and Children. The act did not ban violence outright, but set some limits on the degree of force that could be used. The laws became vaguer still when a child was born outside the sanctity of marriage.

The Victorian legal system was riddled with holes. So, too, was the Crown's case against John Munroe. The key stumbling block was the ambiguous results of the autopsies, specifically that of the child, Ella. While the gunshot wound to the adult skull was irrefutable, even by the defence, no one could pinpoint the cause of the child's demise. Murder was presumed but not proven.[3] There were no obvious signs of violence to the child and, since such souls were vulnerable in the best of circumstances, the Crown could not certify a homicide had taken place. Accordingly, the prosecution filed no murder charges in the death of Ella May Munroe. John Munroe was absolved of any legal consequences for her untimely demise. He would stand trial only for killing Sarah Margaret Vail. There were simply too many questions, and too few protections, for her child. Ella May became a theoretical victim of a hypothetical crime.

Sometimes the best one can hope for is a mere fraction of the retribution due.

NINETEEN

Without Peer, Without Question

The law is a godless religion, consecrated with Latin, commandments, and comfortingly familiar refrains. In 1869 the justice system was a refuge for entrenched thinking, harbouring men who were impervious to change and opposed to the reforms promised by Confederation. It was also a safe haven for those of unexceptional intelligence. One such adequately minded refugee was the Honourable John Campbell Allen, a justice of the Supreme Court of New Brunswick.

Allen was a polarizing figure in the province's judicial sphere. His champions claimed Justice Allen was nice enough, if somewhat impotent. His detractors were far less circumspect. Jeremiah Travis, in his scorched-earth 1884 treatise on the sorry state of New Brunswick jurisprudence, included Allen among the "abject incapables" occupying the province's highest bench. Allen's failings included an indecisiveness that caused him to delay his rulings for "*literally* years." Travis declared Allen "simply a fair lawyer," although he conceded the judge did possess a "kindly disposition."[1] Others begged to differ, at least on the issue of kindness. Allen's own in-laws described him as a "presuming popinjay" and an "impertinent pup,"[2] fighting words among the Victorian elite. Other intimates claimed he was often feisty and temperamental. His well-timed quips from the bench were sarcastic, though seldom cruel.

Allen was born in Kingsclear Parish on October 1, 1817. Details of his youth are hard to come by, but somewhere there were books — shelf upon shelf of verse, theory, and novels, with the occasional atlas thrown in for good measure. Allen inherited his passion for the law from his grandfather Isaac Allen, also a New Brunswick Supreme Court justice. John Allen apprenticed under John Simcoe Saunders, and his meteoric rise to the top of the judicial heap belied both his limited abilities and his intermittently sweet nature.[3]

Allen was selected to preside over the docket's most celebrated case; a fitting choice, as he had a flair for the dramatic. He knew seats in the courtroom would be at a premium. On the morning of the trial's preliminary session, a quick glance out the window revealed the huddled masses yearning to be admitted. Allen abandoned court protocol that spectators be seated and ordered to rise as the judge entered. Justice Allen was never one to stand on ceremony, so neither would his gallery.

At ten a.m. on Tuesday, December 7, 1869, Justice Allen donned his robes and took his place high atop the bench "long before the doors of the Courthouse were thrown open."[4] Seated before him was the entire prosecution team: Crown Counsel W.H. Tuck and Attorney General A.R. Wetmore. The defence table was empty, as was the prisoner's dock. The gallery was also empty, save for a few of the city's better-connected newsmen. All sat in curious silence, confused by the sudden appearance of the judge before the crowds were seated. Quizzical eyes turned to the bench as Allen gave a brief nod to his bailiff, a signal to admit the throng.

As Allen predicted, the crowd surged forward, quickly commandeering every seat. Those lagging behind were left to improvise, using bustles and voluminous skirts to disguise the fact they were crouching on thin air. Allen took it all in, marvelling at this unfiltered glimpse of humanity.[5]

More than twenty minutes passed before the herd was under control,[6] yet the defence table remained conspicuously empty. The judge finally started without them, asking the attorney general if he was "ready to proceed with the trial." Wetmore, eager to tarnish his opponent, replied he was prepared but the court was still "awaiting the arrival of Mr. Thomson." As if on cue, the doors opened to reveal Mr. Jordan, a junior associate in Thomson's legal practice. Jordan hustled to the defence table offering apologies and excuses, assuring Allen, "Mr. Thomson will be here in a few moments."[7] Allen ordered the prisoner to be brought in. As time fillers go, it was a masterful stroke. John Munroe was granted the grand entrance the judge so casually squandered. Captain Francis Jones of the Portland police accompanied him, his uniformed presence lending the prisoner an air of menace. Munroe met the moment with a bemused smile as reporters marvelled how the prisoner "looked calm, indifferent and unchanged."[8]

The untimely arrival of Thomson stole the last of Munroe's thunder. The lawyer offered neither an apology nor an explanation, but launched straight into a motion *in limine*. Thomson demanded the Crown "notify all reporters of newspapers that during the trial of the prisoner, no report of the proceedings shall be published."[9] His argument was simple: "There could be no doubt that the daily publication must tend to mould public opinion, and that most injuriously to the prisoner, as this *ex parte* statements [*sic*] go out before the defence can possibly be heard." It was a bold strategy, for no lawyer had ever requested a publication ban. Thomson addressed his next comments directly to reporters. "He hoped the gentlemen of the press would understand him and that he had no desire to curtail their liberty, but he was satisfied that they would not care to do anything that could possibly operate injuriously against a fellow being, whose life is at stake."[10]

Thomson was not averse to stepping on toes, treading firmly on Sylvester Earle's polished leather oxfords. Thomson said he felt compelled to make this unusual request because the "wholly inadmissible evidence taken before the Coroner, himself quite inexperienced, had been paraded *in extenso*, and accompanied with all sorts of comments highly injurious to the interests of the prisoner."[11] The lawyer's oratory was lean and cadenced, yet the slight was as blunt as a cudgel. Thomson ended with an impassioned plea: "The course of justice must be smooth and regular and no person outside has any right either to accelerate or retard its progress."[12]

John Munroe, rendered mute by the laws of the land, took the unprecedented step of offering a written affidavit to the court, which

Thomson read into the record. Munroe attempted to use his statement to shame the press into silence. He also put in a good word for himself, writing he "could clearly establish his innocence."[13]

The defence's motion won few friends in the press corps, for a full media ban might cost many reporters their jobs. Allen briefly considered the request before ruling. "I am not clear that I have the power," said Allen, "to bring those parties who violate such an order before the Court, and order their punishment and imprisonment. I shall be sorry if the prisoner should be prejudiced in his defence...but I am not satisfied that I can enforce the order."[14] The fourth estate heaved a collective sigh of relief as the motion was denied.

The next order of business was voir dire, the time-honoured and time-consuming process of jury selection. Dozens of potential jurors faced the defence table while the clerk read a statement directly to John Munroe: "These good men are they who shall pass between you and our Sovereign Lady the Queen, and if you would challenge them...you must do so before they are sworn."[15] The clerk need not have worried, for the defence had every intention of challenging them.

The first potential juror on the block was Joseph Maher, a lumber surveyor from Portland.[16] Maher barely drew breath before Thomson leapt to his feet: "I challenge Mr. Maher for cause—that he has made up his mind and expressed an opinion, and I am quite willing to take the Juror's word." Maher happily gave his word. "I have expressed an opinion several times," he said, "that the evidence I have already read in the newspapers was such that, if there was no rebutting evidence, he was guilty."[17] It was the first time anyone openly challenged Munroe's version of events, and the accused fixed Maher with a look that could freeze open water. The judge's decision left many wondering if he was listening. "Mr. Maher was perfectly competent and stands indifferent between the parties," he ruled.[18] Having no other recourse, Thomson used one of his peremptory challenges, and Maher was ordered to stand aside.

Next up was Charles Wilson, a tax collector from Indiantown. Thomson objected to him on sight, citing the reasons given in his prior objection. Allen declared him competent, forcing Thomson to use another of his pre-emptive strikes. The same sequence played out for Thomas Dale and Thomas Logan, as well as eleven other possible triers of fact.[19] Thomson challenged so many men for cause that extra jurors were summoned, forcing the court to trawl the shallow end of the jury pool.

Defence disdain was not the only cause for dismissal. Four men were excused "on the grounds of illness," while John Winters got a free pass for being "over 60 years of age."[20] Ten who were called failed to answer their summons. Luke Stewart, an office clerk, tried to have himself dismissed by pleading the pressing needs of his employment, but the judge would have none of it, and Stewart found himself in the jury box.

The desire to escape jury duty is not of recent origin. Thomas McColgan, the proprietor of Rothesay House, knew exactly which buttons to push. When called, McColgan declared, "I do not think I ought to serve on this jury. I have made up my mind and it cannot be altered."[21] An exhausted Allen replied, "If that is the case, the Juror is not competent." McColgan walked out, delighted to be declared incompetent. Shadrach Holly also decided he "would rather not sit." It was hard to argue that, so Justice Allen did not. To prove his unfitness, Holly announced, "My mind is strongly prejudiced against the prisoner." Allen had no choice but to tell him to step down.

Little by little, the jury box filled, despite all the petty cavils. On more than one occasion the defence strenuously objected to a juror, only to back down when Allen denied the challenge. Each party had just twelve peremptory challenges and the defence saved its objections for the hardest cases.[22] Still, Thomson was nothing if not resourceful, inventing clever alternatives to keep certain men out of the jury box. When Isaac Burpee, the proprietor of the shop in which Munroe purchased the alleged murder weapon, was called as a potential juror, Thomson instantly objected, saying he intended to call Burpee as a witness at trial, thereby exempting him from jury duty.[23] The ploy worked and Burpee was excused, but it was a short-term gain with long-term costs.

Thomson was eventually obligated to call Isaac Burpee to the stand as a character witness. In his brief and haughty testimony, the most Burpee would say on the accused's behalf was that he "came little in contact with him" and therefore "had no opportunity of forming any opinion of his character." When asked about the purchase of the pistol, the ironmonger's answer was so condescending, the court clerk resorted to an italicized font to capture the witness's highly aggrieved tone: "My clerks would know better than *I*, as *I* attend very little to making out orders."[24] Having recorded his contempt for the corrupting influence of retail, Burpee was excused. We are left to wonder whether he would have done more damage to Munroe as a member of the jury.

Fifty-two people were called in order to find the necessary jurors. As the panel was seated and sworn, Munroe surveyed his tribunal—a dozen men with whom he shared nothing but the right to a trial by jury.

Despite his judicial clumsiness, Judge Allen would eventually be knighted by Her Majesty and was appointed Chief Justice of the provincial Supreme Court in 1875. Yet for all his lauded achievements, history would forever link Sir Allen and Munroe, as Allen's entry in the *Canadian Legal Directory* reveals. "Chief Justice Allen has tried many important cases, the most notable of which was the case of John A. Munroe, in 1869, for the murder of Sarah Margaret Vail, whom he seduced. The trial...excited great interest, as the prisoner was in a respectable position in life and was generally supposed to bear a good character."[25]

How wrong history can be.

TWENTY

Victorian Grotesque

With the jury seated, W.H. Tuck opened the case for the Crown. This was, he said, a murder like no other because the accused "is a young man who has occupied a high and respectable position in the community."[1] Tuck reiterated the same point four more times, highlighting the Crown's greatest obstacle to conviction: Munroe simply did not look like a murderer.

Casting the architect in the role of merciless killer demanded more than the usual evidence. Tuck needed to overcome public perceptions of the criminal element. Victorians regarded crime as a moral issue and a question of character.[2] Criminals were considered weak, unable to constrain their primal urges. Evildoers were self-aware and all benighted acts were volitional. Those of poor moral fibre, and this applied almost exclusively to the lower classes, knew right from wrong but believed a life of crime was easier than an honest day's work. These beliefs created an unbreakable syllogism: crime was born of poverty; Munroe was not impoverished; therefore, Munroe could not be a criminal.

Tuck needed to convince the jury that wealth did not prevent murderous rages any more than poverty caused them. He began by breaking the idea into easily digestible nuggets. He told the panel, "It is a solemn and important duty you have to perform," a nod to the death penalty which was the inevitable epilogue to a guilty verdict. "It is true the testimony will be circumstantial," he conceded, "but we find by the books that most of the convictions in criminal cases are from circumstantial evidence."

Circumstances, he argued, were far more telling than social status, for our deeds reveal our true intentions.[3]

Tuck told jurors they must answer four questions, in order, with a simple yes or no: was Mrs. Clarke really Miss Vail; were the remains found on Black River Road those of Miss Vail; was she murdered; and was the murderous act committed by John Munroe? If the answer to any question was no, Munroe was innocent. If, however, the answer to all four questions was yes, the accused was guilty, and the panel would have no choice but to return a unanimous verdict. Tuck assured the jurors that the prosecution would present the evidence necessary to answer each question in the affirmative.

Tuck made good on his word by first addressing the Clarke/Vail conundrum. He called the usual suspects — the coachman Robert Worden and the Lordlys of the Union Hotel — to describe the woman they knew as Mrs. Clarke. The prosecutor then played his trump card: the steamer trunk containing the photo of John Munroe.

To introduce the trunk into evidence, the Crown called baggage handler Albion Neal. He was not the best choice. "I was at that time engaged in handling a good deal of baggage," Neal stated. It was a fair point, for he could hardly be expected to remember a specific trunk more than one year after the fact, and Albion was clearly not one for details. When asked who had checked the luggage, the porter replied, "I don't remember who got me to check the trunk; I think it was a man, though."[4]

On cross-examination, Thomson forced Neal to concede the baggage bore no identifying labels or tags. How, Thomson asked, could he be so sure it was Mrs. Clarke's trunk? The question momentarily stumped Neal. He eventually admitted he did not know who owned the trunk. In his own defence, Neal described the company's luggage handling procedure. "When baggage is brought down, we used to give a duplicate check to the person bringing it and put the other check on the trunk or baggage," he said. "The duplicate check needed to be brought by the person holding it and it entitled him to receive the baggage." The luggage was not stowed by passenger name; the retrieval system relied solely on the matching of claim tags.[5]

The defence gained even more ground when Neal stated, "There might have been a dozen or fifteen trunks in the warehouse unclaimed when this was put in."[6] The assertion was confirmed by a subsequent witness— International Steamship clerk Warren Fletcher—who reported the company had recently "sold forty or fifty packages of unclaimed baggage" and "may have twenty-five on hand now."[7] Using the Crown's own witnesses, the defence rattled the tenuous chain linking Mrs. Clarke to Maggie Vail. Nothing indicated the trunk belonged to someone named Clarke or that John Munroe had checked it. Maggie could have abandoned the trunk at any point during her travels to Boston; there was simply no way to be sure.

Tuck next tried to prove there was no such person as Mrs. Clarke. He called every resident of Black River Road; each swore they knew no one by that name. In the interests of thoroughness, the prosecution called Mr. Thomas Dallon and Mrs. Bridget Connolly. Dallon lived on Black River Road between the Connolly and Collins families, which was all the information Thomas Dallon contributed to the mystery. Less than one minute into his testimony, "the witness showed signs of fainting and was removed to the open air." Judge Allen called for a recess that dragged on for almost an hour, at which point Dallon was "not likely to be able to come forward." Allen ordered a lunch recess.[8]

A good meal seemed to revive Dallon. During the afternoon session he returned to the stand looking slightly peaked. He said that last Hallow's Eve he "was home...hauling hay off the low land and putting it in the barn," placing him in an ideal location to see the crime scene. Dallon coughed, and for a moment everyone feared he would go down again, but he quickly rallied. "I saw no strange woman and child there about that time," Dallon declared, "nor a woman named Clarke or Vail."[9] He was dismissed with the tempered thanks of the court, only to be replaced by Bridget Connolly.

For Bridget Connolly, home would always be Ireland. She was born on the Emerald Isle but eventually traded green waves for blue, making her way across the Atlantic to New Brunswick. She had two sons—John and Henry—and lived out her days in a house she shared with John on the road to Loch Lomond. Mrs. Connolly was a very old woman, paper-skinned and poorly preserved. Indeed, she had no idea how old she was, for taking note of such things seemed frivolous and Bridget was anything but whimsical. She didn't like change and wasn't one for fuss, describing herself as a "poor ould craythur who never stirred from the door."[10] She kept to herself and expected others to do the same.

Connolly was called to the stand because she and her son lived near the site where the bodies were found, but there was no telling her that. Cursed with dementia before the affliction bore Alois Alzheimer's name, Bridget failed to make the link between the location of her house and the crime scene. Mercifully she had been spared the rigours of the coroner's inquest, the police magistrate's examination, and the grand jury deliberations, only to find herself called up for the main trial.

The poor woman took the stand, *non compos mentis*, as the court clerk approached bearing the Holy Bible. Flustered to the point of tears, Connolly "pleaded hard with the crier not to be compelled to take the book, assuring him she had nothing to tell." After repeated placation by the judge and prosecutor, "she reluctantly yielded."[11] When asked if she recalled the events of last Halloween, Connolly whispered she did "not remember last fall."[12] Pressed to clarify if she was at home at the time, her failing memory transposed her home on Black River Road with her ancestral home in Ireland. During a bizarre exchange between the prosecutor and an increasingly agitated witness, it became clear that, when Connolly talked of home, she meant Ireland. The resulting answers were "rather amusing" to court observers.[13]

The defence had even less luck. Thomson asked again if Connolly had any recollection of October 31, 1868. Connolly replied, "I hardly remember one day from another, only I mind my little work — that is all." Thomson asked if she remembered seeing a young woman and child near her home or knew anyone named Clarke or Vail. The compound question proved too much for Bridget, inducing a catatonic state that lasted for several excruciating minutes. Then her face brightened. Confident she finally knew the answer to a question, she declared: "My son's wife who lives near me is a young woman." With that, Bridget Connolly was excused.[14]

TWENTY-ONE

Questions without Answers

Having done all it could to establish the link between Mrs. Clarke and Maggie Vail, the prosecution set about answering the second question: was the body found out on Black River Road that of Miss Vail? Typically, identity was confirmed through visual recognition: someone who knew the deceased looked at and named the body. Since the remains were too decomposed to be recognized, the prosecution used the next best thing: the clothes, hair, and teeth. The Crown was on shaky scientific ground as such details relied solely on the memories of the witnesses. While jurors might reasonably expect Maggie's family to recognize her face, they likely had less faith in the ability of mere acquaintances to recall her wardrobe one year after she went missing.

Jane McLaren, the next witness, tested the prosecution's theory. Like Bridget Connolly, McLaren did not know her age, but thought she was "about twelve years old." Her age and her gender quickly became an issue. She had lived for "about two months with Miss Vail and the child," dressing Ella every day during the spring and summer of 1868. During that time, she said, John Munroe was "the only one who ever called at the house." According to McLaren, the accused came three or four times a week, always in the morning between nine and ten. He never stayed longer than an hour.[1]

McLaren was shown various articles of clothing and identified each one as belonging to either Ella or Maggie. Thomson strenuously objected to her every utterance and, on cross-examination, he attacked the young witness without mercy. He insisted on addressing her as "little girl" and repeatedly implied she had been coached. McLaren was adamant she had not, telling Thomson, "I know what it is to take an oath." The girl's impertinence amused the barrister, who asked the clerk "to note the reply." He then spun on the child, thundering: "Don't you think it is very wrong for a little girl like you to swear that way?" McLaren bore the affront with a calm beyond her years, saying, "O, no sir, it isn't; because it is the truth." Despite the disparity in age, the exchange became a battle of matched wits. When Thomson again insinuated she'd been told what to say, McLaren declared: "No one ever told me that those remains were Miss Vail's. . . . The gentleman I pointed out [John Munroe] is the only one who ever called at the house. . . . What I have sworn to I know and believe, and am not influenced by what I have heard."[2]

Jane McLaren successfully ran Thomson's gauntlet, but the question of identity remained. The prosecution tried again with an older witness. Cynthia F. Dykeman (née Purdy) was thirty-five and married to John, a carpenter and joiner. The couple and their three sons lived in Carleton, where Cynthia worked as a dressmaker.[3] It was a cottage industry for her, as she kept "no store, only a private milliner shop." Dykeman admitted to being "somewhat acquainted with Sarah Margaret Vail," having "made two dresses for her . . . some two years and three or four months or more ago."[4]

Vague recall would be the hallmark of Dykeman's testimony. "I don't remember the materials," she said when asked to describe the dresses. "One was blue, I don't remember the other." To jar her memory Tuck displayed one of the garments recovered from the scene, but the "witness did not want it near her, and seemed unwilling to look at [it] closely." Undeterred, the prosecutor waved the rancid rag under Dykeman's nose as she grew agitated. "I don't recognize it," she cried. "I don't remember the material; I don't remember whether the dress was like that or not." Tuck refused to yield. "Does this resemble the dress you made?" he shouted. "I said I could not tell," she barked back. And with that, Dykeman became a hostile witness.[5]

On cross-examination, Thomson confronted the seamstress with the dress, eliciting a final unambiguous declaration: "I cannot identify the dress."

Another fetid scrap bearing some traces of embroidery was shown, and again "the Witness did not want it near her." The woman's animosity grew, culminating in the following caustic exchange:

> THOMSON: Is that work done by hand?
> DYKEMAN: No, it is done with a needle.
> THOMSON: Is this the same kind of work?
> DYKEMAN: It is crotchet work; a child four years old
> would know one was done with the hook and the other
> with a needle.
> THOMSON: You mean a female child?
> DYKEMAN: I have a male child of that age who could tell
> the difference.
> THOMSON: Which shows the child has been well
> educated.[6]

It seems both the witness and the attorney could be designated as hostile.

Subsequent witnesses also felt the sharp edge of Thomson's tongue. George Johnson Harding came to court at the prosecution's invitation on December 13, 1869. He was a distinguished physician, born, raised, and married in Scotland. Harding and his new wife set sail for New Brunswick, and he had practised in Saint John for almost forty years.[7] For a brief time, he "had a property adjoining Mr. Vail's,"[8] and Maggie was one of his patients.

Harding was as humourless as a mortician. He had been oiled soft with wealth, self-possessed in a way Munroe could only dream of. Harding spoke in a Scottish brogue buffed smooth by four decades in the Maritimes, stating: "My profession is the medical." At that time and place, "the medical" included a primitive form of dentistry. Maggie had visited her neighbour's surgery for an aching tooth "some years ago." The doctor had seen many patients and pulled many teeth, and he could not recall every one. When Harding received his subpoena, he reviewed his records to refresh his memory. "I saw a statement that I did extract a tooth from her," he told the court, "and I tried to recollect." The Crown pressed Harding for specifics. The adult skull recovered from Black River Road had a complete set of teeth except for the left lower second molar. That tooth had been pulled some time before death — enough time for the bone to grow back over the socket — so it was crucial for Harding to recall precisely which tooth he had removed.[9]

Dr. Harding continued to vacillate: "I cannot positively recollect, but I am under the impression —" The defence cut him off in mid-sentence, declaring: "I object to impressions of this kind." Tempers soon flared:

> HARDING: Well, really. I can say no more; but I am under the impression that I did.
> THOMSON: How dare you sir! After I stopped you, force out this statement of what your impression is? Don't you know that a man is on trial for his life?
> HARDING: Really! I can only say what my impression is.
> THOMSON: We don't want your impressions.
> HARDING: Then why was I summoned as a witness at all? I have no direct recollection of this matter.[10]

The witness was ordered to stand down. The prosecution had fumbled the first two of its four questions.

The third question — was it murder? — was straightforward, thanks to Drs. James Christie and LeBaron Botsford. Each took the stand, skull in hand, and described the lethal gunshot, a wound which invariably caused "instantaneous death."[11] Christie also noted the subsequent burial of the body removed all doubt that the wound might be self-inflicted.

The defence scored two points during cross-examination, however. The first was to challenge Christie's competence, forcing the doctor to admit he had "never made any examination of cases where individuals have died from shooting," and that his overall "experience of such cases has been limited."[12]

The defence's second coup came when Thomson returned to the pesky question of identity. According to Phileanor Crear's inquest testimony, she recognized her sister's remains because of the snaggletooth incisor.

Thomson asked both Botsford and Christie if such a feature could serve as the basis of identification. Botsford hesitated. "There is nothing peculiar about the teeth, only they are not regular," he said.[13] Christie's answer raised far more doubt: "There is nothing very remarkable about the tooth which overlaps—there are many such; I see a person in front of me there now who has just such a one." Christie dug in deeper, adding, "In this case, the tooth overlaps to the right—that is only peculiar in this particular case because there might be another of exactly the same peculiarity."[14] Thomson paused to allow jurors to decipher the doctor's statement.

Looking to exploit Christie's inexperience, Thomson asked a final question regarding the body's state of decomposition. Christie had no expertise in this particular area, but Thomson wagered the doctor's ego would compel him to answer. The defence lawyer formulated a question linking the rate of decay to the timeline of the murder affixed to his client. It was a well-laid trap, and Christie walked blithely into it. "If the body had been buried there under the moss in October 1868, and never been disturbed until the time the remains were found, there would certainly be decomposed matter remaining," he stated.[15] In other words, if Maggie died at Munroe's hand on October 31, 1868, Christie was certain more flesh would be present when the body was discovered in September 1869. The foolhardy conjecture brought a smile to Thomson's face as he dismissed the witness.[16]

The defence gained further ground from another key prosecution witness: John M. Marshall. Marshall was chief of police for the city of Saint John, a post he had occupied for the past seven years. He was also a childhood friend of John Munroe and "had been intimate with his family for years."[17] Marshall once visited Munroe's home on Charlotte Street, where he met Annie Munroe and the couple's first child.

Marshall volunteered to assist during the architect's arrest at Craft's public house, escorting Munroe to the police magistrate's office, alongside Portland police chief Francis Jones. Marshall freely stated he had cautioned his friend, telling Munroe, "You had better not say anything to anybody."[18] Munroe ignored the advice.

Chief Marshall admitted he did not record what Munroe said to him, a major misstep for which Thomson berated him at length. The defence also took Marshall to task for what he did after Munroe made his statement.

> MARSHALL: I did go down stairs and told the Police
>   Magistrate part of the circumstances.
> THOMSON: Then you consider you done that as a friend?
> MARSHALL: I did.
> THOMSON: Then God save the poor victim who may be
>   hereafter subjected to your friendship.[19]

Marshall squirmed in the dock as the defence tried to put words in his mouth. Asked Thomson: "Did you not say 'Now John, if there is any person in whom you should have confidence, it should be in me. I have been acquainted with you and your family and the whole connection was so long that you ought to have confidence in me. Now do tell me, in confidence, the whole of this unfortunate affair.' Now sir, did you or did you not use that language?" The question was convoluted, but Marshall's answer was simple: "I did not." Thomson did not care about the reply, seeking only to get Munroe's version of events on the record. Since the prisoner could not speak, Thomson took every opportunity to testify for him.[20]

Thomson continued to hammer the witness. "Do you or do you not, when prisoners are in custody, endeavour to extract information from them in the way of conversation, and then use it against them afterwards?" he demanded. The insinuation angered the police chief, who replied emphatically: "I do not." Thomson's tactics had yet to draw censure from the bench, so he risked asking a follow-up question: "Did you not, the same afternoon he was arrested, meet old Mr. Munroe on Chipman's Hill and say 'John, I am very sorry for this unfortunate affair, but I will keep you posted up in everything. Whatever John says to me will be in perfect confidence and no action will be taken upon it'?" Marshall was adamant he "did not use such words, or anything like it."[21]

The attorney general finally objected to the line of questioning, and Thomson objected to the objection. The opposing parties squabbled back and forth until Justice Allen ruled Thomson's questions were not "proper."[22] Thomson took offense; in a huff he announced he would "not continue the cross examination if the objection be taken"[23] and reclaimed his seat beside the accused, a perfectly matched set of men wronged.

The attorney general rose to redirect, giving Marshall the opportunity to choose his own words. The witness tried to restore his tarnished reputation. "I feel it to be my duty, when a crime such as this has been committed in the community, to use my best endeavours to ferret out the guilty party, and instruct my policemen to do the same," he said, "and I have done so in this instance."[24] On that note, the prosecution rested its case.

Reporters depicted Marshall as duplicitous and conniving. Pity poor John Munroe, they wrote, for in his hour of need he turned to a trusted friend and was betrayed. Thanks to Thomson's efforts, reasonable doubt was setting in.

TWENTY-TWO

Evidence of Character, Character as Evidence

When Thomson rose to present Munroe's defence, his greatest hindrance was the law itself. The court was unaccustomed to a proactive defence, because the burden of proof rested entirely with the prosecution. In 1869 the overwhelming majority of defendants appeared without counsel. On those rare occasions when the accused was represented, the lawyer was largely decorative and toothless. Munroe's trial was a test case of sorts, for he intended to prove Munroe's innocence. His strategy was two-pronged: first, convince the court Maggie was still alive, and second, demonstrate that Munroe's unimpeachable character made him incapable of murder.

To that end, the defence summoned thirty-seven witnesses to the stand. Of these, thirty-five were called solely as character witnesses. Thomson's strategy was fundamentally flawed. Even the most lenient jurist could not consider these witnesses unbiased or impartial. Twenty were former business associates of John Munroe, contractors who relied on the accused for their livelihood. To a man, they swore they barely knew the prisoner, although he seemed harmless enough. Three of the witnesses were employees of John Munroe Sr. All three confided under oath they were compensated for their testimony. Six character witnesses were neighbours and family members, including the parents of the accused.

The first Munroe to the stand was John Sr., who proudly declared: "I am the father of the prisoner at the bar." He insisted his son "was doing very well; his business has been increasing very fast; he was in no pecuniary embarrassment at all." Thomson allowed the witness free rein, with little prompting or editing. J.J. Munroe then launched into a spit-soaked tirade against John Marshall. Marshall told him anything his son said "would be in strict confidence and no action would be taken upon it," Munroe claimed. "I did meet Mr. Marshall on the very night my son was arrested and the words I have stated are just what passed between us," he insisted.[1]

Thomson introduced an entirely new line of questioning, asking about a man named George Wade. Wade would figure prominently in the day's testimony even though the man himself never set foot in the courthouse. John Sr. told the court he'd recently brought Wade in from the United States, at his own rather considerable expense, with the expectation Wade would "give evidence favourable" to the accused.[2] But an ugly accusation was making the rounds in the press: several papers reported John Sr. paid Wade to perjure himself.

Such revelations might have derailed a lesser lawyer, but Thomson simply used Munroe Sr. to get the desired testimony on the record. In a blaze of hearsay, he detailed the encounter Wade had been called, and perhaps paid, to recount. "He told me that he had been in the habit of carrying letters for John over to this Miss Vail, in Carleton, he also said he carried a parcel from John down to the boat on Hallow E'en, and gave it to Miss Vail," Munroe testified. "This he said in the presence of my wife, my mother and my daughter. This statement he made voluntarily."[3] Attorney General Wetmore's objections filled the courtroom, but it was too late. The jury heard the account, and the prosecution's protests could not scrub it from their memories.

Thomson finished with the witness then took his seat, casting a wry smile at Wetmore. The attorney general rose to cross-examine, but first he did a little testifying of his own. He reminded the jury that Wade was one of the employees at Munroe's luggage factory, leaving it to the panel to connect the dots. When pressed, John Sr. admitted Wade was in his home the previous night although, he insisted, "I did not tell him any evidence I wished him to give."[4] Wetmore's contemptuous snort left little doubt as to the validity of the statement.

In numerous sidebars with the judge, Thomson and Wetmore debated the merits of putting George Wade on the stand. Thomson argued Wade must be allowed to testify, because Wetmore opened the door by grilling the prisoner's father regarding Wade's statements. "By strict rule of law," Thomson railed, "I was in consequence entitled to get out the whole facts."[5] Wetmore, however, refused to summon Wade, arguing that Thomson had introduced Wade's statements as hearsay. After much back and forth, the judge ruled in favour of the prosecution.

Thomson later posed a rhetorical question that expressed his disdain for the ruling: "If Wade did pretend that he saw the young woman in the boat, and did take Munroe's money when in reality he had not seen her, what must be thought of him, what must be thought of his character?"[6] Thomson always brought the debate back to the question of character. The elder Munroe stepped down, having done all the law would allow to save his son.

Vanity cast deep roots in the Munroe family tree. Mary Eleanor Munroe was still spry at age fifty-one.[7] She perpetually sported fashions better suited to a woman twenty years her junior, and though she once possessed a curdled beauty, her recent maternal fretting had gouged deep lines in her face. Mary Munroe entered the court and took her place in the witness chair. She choked back a sob when she spied her son in the prisoner's dock.[8]

She began with her identity: "I am mother of the prisoner."[9] It would be the only full sentence she would utter. Thomson had called her to recount the conversation she overheard between her husband and George Wade, but the attorney general objected, saying her testimony was hearsay and therefore inadmissible. Thomson conceded "that, strictly speaking, this was inadmissible evidence but he did not think that, under the circumstance, the Attorney General would have objected to it."[10] Thomson thought wrong, and Wetmore refused to withdraw his objection. Judge Allen decided the court would hear nothing more from Mrs. Munroe, including her testimony as to her son's character.[11] That a mother loved her child and believed him to be incapable of murder was a biological imperative. Allen felt certain no one actually needed to hear her say it. Mary Munroe stepped down in tears.

Thomson had done all he could to paint the accused as a decent, upstanding citizen. When he rose again, it was to prove Maggie Vail was still alive. In an ideal world, the barrister would have orchestrated a melodramatic denouement in which Miss Vail burst into the courtroom with little Ella in her arms, forcing the prosecution to grovel for forgiveness. Since such theatrics were not an option, Thomson worked with what he had, and what he had were two very questionable witnesses: William Howard and George Hicks.

William Howard earned his living, when he could, with the strength of his back and hands. Labourers of Howard's stripe were normally beneath the notice of gentlemen like John Munroe, but the two men knew each other well. Howard graciously offered his services to the defence, having "voluntarily" come forward with information of great importance.[12]

Howard had been working at the Round House near the steamboat wharf at the time Maggie went missing, and he lived right around the corner. On his days off he liked to "go down to see the boat go away," the Maritime equivalent of trainspotting. On "a dark, wet morning," Howard was standing in his usual spot at the head of the wharf when he saw John Munroe engaged in a conversation with another man. Howard watched as Munroe boarded the ship to rendezvous with Maggie Vail, who was waiting at the bow, holding Ella. The three eventually went below deck. Howard "saw nothing of them after that." He was "positive [Munroe] went downstairs in the boat — I can't be mistaken on that point." He recalled "well what the child had on." She was nestled in Maggie's "left arm" and "had on a red and white Berlin hood."[13]

On cross-examination the attorney general pushed Howard for details, specifically what time the boat pulled away and the height of the tide when it sailed. The witness answered without hesitation, giving a precise description of the conditions as the ship departed. With a smirk, Wetmore flipped through the pages of the *Farmer's Almanac* to the entry for

November 2, 1868, the day Maggie and Ella supposedly set sail for Boston. According to the almanac, Howard's description of high tide was off by more than four hours. The witness bristled at the suggestion and "persisted in saying he was not mistaken. He could not tell whether it was November or October that he saw this take place, but he was satisfied it was on a Monday morning."[14] Wetmore happily let the remark stand.

William Howard's curious blend of absolute certainty and complete ambiguity could not be salvaged, despite Thomson's best efforts at damage control. The defence excused Howard, hoping to regain lost ground with its final witness, George Hicks.

Like life, George Hicks was nasty, brutish, and short. A dark, unkempt beard offset his alehouse complexion. Even when seated Hicks was in constant motion, his restless Adam's apple bobbing incessantly in his throat. On any given weekend, he was prone to bar fights, living a life dedicated to the complete avoidance of both disaster and fortune. He was also an accomplished liar.[15]

Hicks slumped into the witness box, raising his right hand as if its position alone were a hedge against perjury. It soon became clear his answers would benefit neither the prosecution nor the defence. With each question, he tilted his head like a dog awaiting a command it might finally understand. Thomson did his best to guide him as Hicks wended a tortuous route through his narrative. He started by describing Maggie Vail. "I think she resembled her sister...a good deal," he said. "She might be taller and she mightn't be as tall. I couldn't say." Her hair, he said, "was yellow. I didn't mean yellow. That was not my evidence. I said light. If you can make a meaning out of it, I can't."[16]

Thomson tried calling Hicks's attention to the morning of Monday, November 2, 1868, the day Munroe claimed to have seen Maggie and Ella off on the boat. The defence lobbed Hicks a soft ball by including the day and date in the question, but he missed the pitch entirely. Twice he insisted it was "a Saturday night" when he saw Maggie on the wharf. Thomson rephrased the question, asking Hicks if he recalled seeing Miss Vail near the steamer.

HICKS: I did not see her go on board the boat. I wouldn't swear too positive it was her because it was a long time since I saw her.

THOMSON: When you saw her at the time, whom did you suppose her to be?

HICKS: I didn't suppose my head about her at the time, because I had very little acquaintance with her, but I came to think afterwards who she was, and I arrived at the conclusion that she was Miss Vail...I wouldn't be too sure of it.[17]

During cross-examination, Wetmore pressed the issue again. Poor Hicks crumpled, saying he "wouldn't be too sure that she went on the steamer, and won't swear it was Miss Vail." At this point, the court stenographer abandoned all efforts to record the dialogue, capturing his frustration with the notation: "The question was frequently repeated, and he always said he would not swear."[18]

Hicks perjured himself repeatedly in a single breath: "I was certainly on the wharf on Nov. 2nd. I was not up there from October 27th to November 9th. I came down on Saturday night; I did not swear that I would not say that it was on Saturday night I came down."[19]

The endless double negatives and retractions left jurors bewildered, sighing in disgust. Hicks then segued into an indecipherable tangent about working for a man named Charlton, contradicting his statement that he was near the wharf in the late fall of 1868. Long past caring, Wetmore was about to abandon the cause when a particular set of Hicks's synaptic misfires caught his ear. Hicks was questioning his own testimony regarding Maggie's physical appearance: "I can't say whether she wore a hat or bonnet. I only noticed what the baby wore, that she had a Berlin hood. I have been in Court pretty much all the time."[20] The inadvertent admission stopped Wetmore cold. Witnesses were not permitted in court prior to testifying, as the statements of others might influence them. Wetmore wondered what else Hicks might let slip.

The prosecutor casually asked how Hicks came to be a witness in the case. Hicks replied that he had worked at Munroe's trunk factory for about eighteen months but was let go. When Hicks heard about Munroe's son during the inquest, he approached "a man named Kilpatrick, who takes John's dinner to him." Hicks told Kilpatrick he had information, and Kilpatrick relayed the message to Munroe Sr. After he agreed to testify on John Munroe's behalf, Hicks was immediately put back on the payroll at the trunk factory. [21]

Wetmore then asked Hicks to explain the time lag between when he first saw the woman on the wharf and the moment he decided that woman was Maggie Vail. Hicks's response did little to clarify the matter: "I don't think it was six months after; I don't think it was three months, or as much as two months. It wasn't a bother at all. It may be about six months. I can't say whether I was at work or not at the time. I was in St. John at the time. I can't say that either, for I sometimes went away." Wetmore cast a bewildered look at the jury, shrugged, and took his seat. [22]

Thomson rose to redirect, but Hicks was frantic, no longer able to answer even the simplest of questions. Instead, Thomson testified on Hicks's behalf, posing a question so leading no modern-day judge would allow it. Thomson asked whether Hicks recognized the person walking with Miss Vail. Hicks had previously sworn Maggie was alone when he saw her on the wharf, but the defence hoped the jury had overlooked this detail in the avalanche of nonsense that followed. Thomson laid out his breadcrumbs so neatly even Hicks could follow them, and the resulting testimony seemed almost plausible. Suddenly Hicks recalled seeing a woman named Mary Alice Jenkins walking with Maggie on the pier. With further coaching from Thomson, Hicks picked up the trail.

> HICKS: I knew Mary Alice Jenkins intimately, and seeing a
> stranger with her, I asked who she was ... it is a habit to
> ask who persons are whom you see walking with one you
> know. . . . The face seemed familiar. That was what caused
> me to reflect on it afterwards. . . . I first mentioned this to
> Kilpatrick. This was after the inquest.

THOMSON: Then it struck you that this girl that was
   supposed to be murdered was the girl you saw going
   down the wharf?
HICKS: From hearing Mr. Munroe's story, I was led to
   reflect on the subject.[23]

This was as good as it was likely to get, so Thomson discharged the witness. Hicks's bizarre turn left the court exhausted and confused. Judge Allen took pity on the jurors and called it a day.

TWENTY-THREE

"A Man Steeped to the Lips in Crime"

Samuel Thomson greeted the final day of testimony with a mental palate cleanser, a character witness called solely to remind the jury of the inherent decency of the accused. The choice was not without controversy, for the witness had caused a ruckus the day before. As George Hicks imploded in the dock, a shingle maker named John H. Miles tried to enter the courtroom. The gallery was already filled to capacity, and the constables refused to admit Miles,[1] who unleashed a wail of protest normally reserved for poorly anaesthetized surgical patients. Thomson intervened, assuring Miles he would be first on the stand the following day. On December 16, Miles returned full of righteous indignation. He placed his hand upon the Bible as if he had written it, declaring he would tell the truth, with God's help of course.

Miles launched into an autobiography that was neither brief nor relevant, the only salient point being his twenty-six-year-long acquaintance with the prisoner. When asked to describe Munroe's character, the witness mulled the question like fine wine before issuing his decree: "As far as I know, he was always mild and inoffensive. I never saw anything vicious in him. Was much surprised when I heard he was arrested. I could not believe it." He was not the only one. When offered the opportunity to cross-examine, Attorney General Wetmore dismissed the witness with a wave of his hand, refusing to give the man's testimony any credibility by questioning it. Miles's face registered his shock, and for a second time he was shown the courthouse door.[2]

The defence had one last witness listed, although Thomson did everything in his power to keep the man off the stand. Instead, he asked to read a telegram received the night before; the prosecution objected. Much legal wrangling ensued as Thomson tried repeatedly to read the communiqué for the jury. A second telegram spontaneously appeared, allegedly from the same source, but the defence still could not get its contents admitted into the record. Finally, the judge declared, "The only way Mr. Thomson could now put any fact before the court was by affidavit." Only then did Thomson reveal the telegram's author was present in the courtroom.[3] As Wetmore rolled his eyes in disbelief, the defence called Edward Price to the stand.

Price was a farmer from Sussex. His hair was freshly barbered for the occasion, revealing a band of virgin white skin that traced his face like an x-ray. His clothes were coarse homespun, cut for function without a thought for fashion. He approached the bench with hat literally in hand, nodding deference to Judge Allen. He never spoke above a low mumble as he recalled a day in the late fall one year prior when he and his son were travelling to Saint John along the head of Loch Lomond. When they reached the fingerboards at The Forks, they encountered a woman and "a very small child." The woman said she'd tried to catch the mail coach into town but had missed it, so she offered to pay Price if he would drive her. The farmer agreed, and the pair climbed into the buggy.[4]

Price's account came piecemeal as the prosecution objected time and again, arguing that any recounting of the conversation between Price and Vail was hearsay. Thomson advised the witness to restrict his comments solely to his own impressions, and Price followed his lead. "My impression is she called herself Mrs. Clarke," he said. "I am a poor hand at describing. She was a lowish sized woman, dressed in dark clothes...I don't know any more...The child had something like a tippet and a Berlin hood of white and red on its head. We talked all the way in."[5]

The timing of the trip was crucial, yet Price skated the issue. On cross-examination, Wetmore pressed him for an exact date. The witness could not recall the month, much less the day, of the trip. His sole point of reference was "the big storm that remained right on," a meaningless detail in a land plagued by inclement weather. Wetmore let the matter rest, and Price stepped down.[6]

The case had run its course. Both sides had exhausted their arguments and their pools of witnesses. All that remained was to offer their closing summations to the jury and await the verdict. Thomson rose first for the defence.

Truth is an abrasive word, and the defence used it liberally to burnish away any defects in Munroe's story. It was the truth, Thomson said, that "even the hunted hare is not run to earth without a fair start." Yet in this case, he observed, "the law officers of the crown seemed determined to fasten their bloody fangs at once on the prisoner, and at all hazards send him to the scaffold." Truth could also be found in the "monstrous" and "most unsatisfactory state" of the province's criminal justice system, which routinely "put men in the dock; bound hand and foot, compelling them to be silent while their lives are sworn away." His client's inability to speak in his own defence galled Thomson, who asked jurors: "If against one of your own children a complaint were made by another child, would you condemn it unheard?" Of course not, Thomson bellowed, for to do so would be a gross dereliction of "duty to yourself, your child and your country."[7]

Thomson's ten-thousand-word closing argument stretched for more than three hours, and the numbers are telling. He invoked the Lord's name on twenty-two occasions but only mentioned the Crown seven times. He pleaded for the jury to have mercy no fewer than ten times. By far the most impressive statistic was his use of the rhetorical question, Thomson's favoured mode of argument. In quick-fire succession he posed eighty-one questions without answers, among them: "Would not a guilty man have removed all the clothes from the remains?" and "Can you imagine that this young man, standing high in his profession, overwhelmed with business, netting $3000 to $4000 a year, would take away life for such a sum as $500?"[8]

Before the jurors could formulate their answers, Thomson redirected their attention to the accused. Placing his hand on his client's shoulder, Thomson conceded that Munroe was an adulterer, but he was no killer. He was simply a man who fell prey to a "determined" woman. Maggie Vail was desperate, and with no other viable candidate on offer, she set her sights on John Munroe. Any man would be powerless in such circumstances, and no man could reasonably expect his client to withstand such temptation.[9]

Once again, the case boiled down to the question of character. "Guilt," Thomson declared, "always hides its head," yet the accused did no such thing. Indeed, the architect went about his business, "showing no uneasiness or trepidation or alteration in his manner." "Surely," the defence continued, "his previous character should plead for him." Thomson pointed to his client as he posed his eighty-second rhetorical query: "Will you say that he was a man steeped to the lips in crime?" Of course not, Thomson declared, for the architect was not "callous." He was a devoted son, husband, and father, a pillar of the community. Such men were incapable of darkness. On that note, the defence rested.[10]

Wetmore stood to address the panel, clearly bemused by his opponent's performance. He assured the jury his summary would be brief and much less fraught. The prisoner was indeed a husband and a father. The attorney general then asked a rhetorical question of his own: "If the prisoner had had any regard for those ties, would he have maintained for years an illicit connection with this woman . . . forgetting the partner of his bosom and the children of his loins in the arms of a paramour?"[11]

As for Munroe's legally mandated silence, Wetmore opined: "It has been argued at great length that the prisoner should be heard in his own case, and that great injustice is done because he is not allowed to give evidence; but many able men say that this would be the greatest cruelty. . . . Such is the mercy of English law." He offered a glimpse of a future that has since come to pass. "Suppose that law was altered and the prisoner did not choose to give evidence?" he asked. "Would not the irresistible conviction then be that he was guilty?"[12]

Wetmore offered answers to many of his opponent's hypothetical questions. The defence argued there was no motive, yet the Crown saw plenty of reasons for Munroe to act. Munroe, Wetmore argued, "had a wife and children, a character for sobriety," and "was rising in his profession"; but "this girl was dogging him and demanding money of him; that he could not offer her a home and that he dreaded the effect exposure must have upon his business.... Is there a man in the world who would not give any earthly possession to get rid of such an intolerable burden?" Thomson belaboured the fact Munroe had surrendered to authorities, which he argued was the act of an innocent man. Wetmore saw it differently. "He might have thought the remains were so decayed as to be incapable of being identified," he argued, or perhaps Munroe believed "his standing in the community" would protect him.[13]

Finally, the attorney general reached the crucial question of character. "Evidence as to the prisoner's good previous character has been much relied on," he said, "but where is there a man who at some time or another has not possessed a good character? Every man has one until he forfeits it." Wetmore reminded the panel that "evidence of character amounts to little against the positive evidence that a murder was committed." And, to the prosecutor's mind, there could be no doubt a murder was committed: "I maintain that in all the annals of crime there never was a case in which circumstantial evidence was so cogent."[14]

If the defence wanted to make it all about character, the Crown would readily oblige. "It was said that none but a madman would have chosen such a place; none but a madman would perpetrate such a crime," Wetmore said, tossing Thomson's well-chosen words back across the aisle. He agreed with his esteemed colleague that the murders had been the act of a madman, but Wetmore had no problem seeing Munroe as that madman. "Like most men and villains," the prosecutor concluded, John Munroe's good traits did not absolve him of his brutal acts. Wetmore allowed the thought to linger as he took his seat.[15]

The closing statements consumed the entire day. It was just after five o'clock when Wetmore finished his summation, leaving the jurors tired and queasy. They requested a break until the following morning, which Judge Allen granted. As his gavel dropped, "the throng of Barristers and others was so great that some minutes elapsed after the adjournment before the Jury could leave the box or the prisoner be remanded."[16]

On December 17, 1869, Judge Allen opened the session with his instructions to the jury. "Crime always seeks concealment," Allen cautioned, reminding his panel not to be fooled by Munroe's calm exterior. He also warned that "human memory and eyes and ears are fallible." The judge made an example of Mary Ann Lordly, suggesting "this whole story was the coinage of her imagination."[17] The judge had equally harsh words for John Munroe Sr. and his paid witnesses. Allen's thoughts and opinions filled the better part of five hours. At two o'clock, Allen released the jury to begin its deliberations. Inside the courtroom, spectators anxiously awaited the verdict; outside, "little knots of people" filled the streets, offering their insights and conjecture.[18]

Less than one hour later, word came of a verdict. As the jurors filed into their box, "every face wore a painful solemn look."[19] John Munroe was escorted to the dock looking "pale and haggard and very anxious." He "gazed mechanically about, with that restless yet steady stare which had become familiar during this trial."[20]

A speedy verdict typically favoured the defence. Thomson stood beside his client, already jubilant for a job well done. Justice came swiftly indeed as Allen ascended the bench and the jury foreman read the verdict: "GUILTY, with strong recommendation to mercy."[21] The reporter for the *Daily Morning News* captured the scene that followed:

> At these words, every eye fell upon the prisoner, and he, seemingly stunned for a moment, did not appear fully to comprehend the import, and when the truth broke fully upon his mind, his head seemed to sink spasmodically between his shoulders, and burying his face in his hands

and prostrating himself upon the seat of the dock, his whole frame shook with convulsive agony. . . . Not a word — not a sound — not a movement was seen or heard elsewhere than in that fatal dock, and tears rolled down many cheeks as they saw the man who had carried himself so defiantly through the many scenes of this terrible tragedy at last subdued by the majesty of the law and appalled at the prospect of death.[22]

John Munroe's wealth and privilege had not saved him. The architect was a convicted killer. Though he had yet to be sentenced, there was little question as to how it would all end.

ACT FOUR

In which the role of character refuses to die.

TWENTY-FOUR

The Voice of Reason, the Voice of the People

Edward Willis, the managing editor of Saint John's *Daily Morning News*, could scarcely believe his ears. The verdict was an unconscionable miscarriage of justice, and the jurors were clearly fools. John A. Munroe was no more a murderer than the Queen herself, a fact Willis would have sworn to had they afforded him the opportunity.

Willis was a man of many opinions, all of them tightly held and liberally shared. Fortunately, life handed him a series of jobs designed to give voice to those opinions: editor and shareholder of one of the city's premier dailies, a seat in the House of Assembly, and, in the not so distant future, postmaster of Saint John.[1] He was also a Mason, an Anglican, and an Orangeman, labels he wore with pride and a certain degree of defensive bluster.[2] Not bad for the son of an Irish immigrant who was all of thirty-four when Munroe's jury delivered its cockeyed verdict.

Willis stormed from the county courthouse, strong-arming his way through the throng. His ears caught snippets of conversation as he passed. The consensus was Munroe had been wronged. The convicted man's father was already setting up a soapbox on the courthouse steps, shouting his son's innocence to the reporters hastily assembling at his feet. The elder Munroe came prepared. In his hand he brandished a petition demanding the immediate reversal of the verdict and implored all who passed to sign it. Just as Willis rounded the corner, bound for his office, John Munroe

Sr. announced his plan to deliver the petition personally into the hands of the Governor General. The promise was met with cheers.

Thundering along the avenue, Willis bristled at the state of the province's legal system. The courts were temples of ineptitude where justice was found only in the loop of a hangman's noose. Willis fervently believed patricians like John Munroe deserved better. He had never met the architect, but few things riled him more than injustice (although those who opposed Confederation or supported separate Catholic schools ran a close second).[3] Willis did not know how the woman and child met their tragic end on Black River Road, but he felt certain it was not by Munroe's hand. The jury may have overlooked the obvious signs of Munroe's innocence, but Willis could not.

Edward put pen to paper then nailed his thesis to the cathedral door, in a prominently placed editorial that filled most of the day's late edition. He consolidated his argument into five points. First, Munroe's gentle and gentile nature: "The disposition which would render such a crime possible on the part of Munroe seemed to be wholly wanting in him: He is known here from boyhood, and the evidence of his naturally mild, gentle, amiable disposition was clear and conclusive. To all human appearances, a man less likely to commit such a deed as that charged upon him did not exist in New Brunswick."[4]

Second, lack of motive. "There was no motive conceivable apparently strong enough to lead a man of Munroe's position to perpetrate such a crime," Willis wrote. "If he desired to break off his connection with her, he had but to provide for the child and keep away from its mother and the wish would be attained." Munroe was a philandering husband saddled with a volatile mistress and a bastard child, but that, in the editor's educated opinion, was not reason enough to kill. That he had not ended their affair was evidence of its robust state. Willis was equally certain money was not the root of this evil: "If [the motive] was to get or keep the poor girl's money, this supposition seemed to be repulsed by the fact that Munroe was suffering no penury embarrassment, that he was in receipt of a large yearly income and that he was living in a plain and inexpensive manner."[5]

Willis's third point addressed the architect's mental acumen: Munroe was simply too brilliant to have committed the crime as perpetrated. "A man of Munroe's intelligence and cleverness would not perform the dreadful deed close by the Black River Road, in the middle of the day," he argued. No, if Munroe had wanted them dead, he would have found a better location.[6]

His fourth point highlighted Munroe's knowledge of the region. The architect's ancestral home was on Black River Road. It therefore stood to reason he would not have disposed of the bodies in that place in such a manner. Munroe knew locals traversed those woods in search of berries, firewood, and other resources. Furthermore, it was incomprehensible that so clever a man "would make no efforts to remove at least the clothing in which the bodies had been buried, which might lead to identification if found."[7]

Finally, there were Munroe's actions in the aftermath of the crime. "It seemed highly improbable that a guilty man would stay as Munroe did," Edward Willis argued, "quietly pursuing his ordinary avocations near the Court House for some days after the inquest commenced its investigations."[8]

Having exalted Munroe's virtues, the *Daily Morning News* attacked the prosecution's case and the witnesses' credibility. The editorial highlighted the fact that victim identification was basely on clothing, a method that "was far from being conclusive" and relied on testimony that "was given with a positiveness and confidence which...was unwarranted and such as no calm and discriminating person would offer." In conclusion, Willis wrote, "These considerations involved strong probabilities in favour of Mr. Munroe's innocence and they could be neutralized only by probabilities of the greatest possible force and weight pointing to an opposite conclusion." Such probabilities were not met; therefore, Munroe was an innocent man.[9]

For all its cool reasoning, Willis's editorial was an emotionally charged argument based on assumptions of Munroe's character, intelligence, and motives. It was also unprecedented. Newspaper accounts of the time consistently painted those accused (and certainly those convicted) as cold-blooded blackguards. For a leading publication to stake its reputation in defence of a convicted murderer was extraordinary. It was also foolhardy, for Munroe had done nothing to warrant such support, save for being well off.

John Munroe's legal odyssey moved to the sentencing phase on Tuesday, December 21. By two o'clock that afternoon, more than fifteen hundred people had assembled in front of the courthouse. In the throng were judges, barristers, newspaper editors, and other dignitaries who expected to be admitted, but "they were not to enjoy any privileges not extended to other enlightened citizens." Seating was strictly allocated on a first-come basis. When the doors opened, the mob rushed up the stairs pell-mell, the "demands of morbid curiosity" destroying the solemnity of the court. Inside the courtroom, "a disorderly crowd, composed largely of boys, entered with noisy exclamations and in their haste broke down the wings of the baize door." [10] The throng settled as the prisoner, "looking very much broken down," was escorted in. His eyes never left the floor, and "his countenance wore the expression of one from whom all hope had fled."[11]

Justice Allen asked Munroe if he had anything to say before sentence was passed. It was the only time a defendant was permitted to address the court, but Munroe refused to speak. Allen sighed and declared, "It becomes my painful duty to move that the just judgement of the law be passed upon him." The judge could not hide his compassion for the prisoner, telling Munroe, "I shall not refer to anything that might wound your feelings." He reminded the spectators in the gallery that the jury had recommended mercy, and he concurred. Unfortunately, the decision was not in Allen's hands. "While I shall take care to forward this recommendation to His Excellency the Governor General," he cautioned Munroe, "I cannot hold out the slightest hope that the prerogative of mercy will be exercised in your case."[12]

Judge Allen distanced himself still further before passing sentence—"not my sentence, but that which the law directs"—upon Munroe. Allen was visibly distraught as he ordered Munroe to be taken to the place of execution and, on Tuesday February 15, 1870, hanged by the neck until dead. Munroe never once lifted his eyes from the floor.[13]

At the drop of his gavel, bedlam ensued as reporters and spectators swarmed the prisoner. John Munroe Sr. fought for one last word with his son, but he was thwarted at every turn.

On the morning of January 21, 1870, Governor General John Young stood at his office window in Rideau Hall. Only the second person to fill the post, Young was still getting his bearings. The Governor General's vague mandate was to serve as the representative of the British monarch within Canada's nascent parliamentary democracy. Less than twelve months in, many in that parliament thought Young was simply making it up as he went along.[14]

Born in Bombay but of Irish descent, Young had been marked for greatness since infancy. In his heyday he "was not shy about voicing criticism or strong opinions," causing those criticized to resent "his independent mind."[15] That morning, age sixty-two, his waning energies had shifted from empire building to securing his own legacy. He was tired and ready to retire, although the opportunity to do so would elude him for two more years.

The ambiguity of the governor general's portfolio suited Young, who was a lawyer by trade. He had been called to the bar in 1834 yet had limited experience in the practise of law, rarely setting foot in a courtroom.[16] This was of little concern for, as one of his successors later quipped, a governor general needed only "the patience of a saint, the smile of cherub, the generosity of an Indian prince and the back of a camel."[17] Young perused his morning's assignations and recognized the name of his first visitor. Given his guest's well-publicized nature, Young realized that, while his fluency in law might prove beneficial, he would need those other attributes far more.

John Munroe Sr. had made the long and arduous journey to Ottawa to plead on his son's behalf. The elder Munroe rarely prostrated himself before his betters—largely because he did not believe he had any—but his son was scheduled to hang in less than a month. The family patriarch was willing to make an exception. Munroe carried with him two crucial dispatches. The first was the petition asking Young to overturn his son's conviction or, at the very least, commute his sentence to life imprisonment. The plea bore more than two thousand signatures, including those of many eminent figures in Maritime politics and commerce.[18] Munroe personally coerced every man he knew to sign the document and when the font of male petitioners ran dry, he recruited signatures from the wives and dowagers of New Brunswick's elite.[19]

Munroe also clutched newspaper clippings lamenting his son's wrongful conviction. Topping the pile was the *Daily Morning News*, which rebuked the high court for condemning a man who "must have been bereft of his senses."[20] Many in the press believed John A. Munroe was a visionary architect who had not yet paid the debt his genius owed the world. Munroe Sr. downplayed the fact that the press had also argued the wording of his petition "was not considered expressive of the feelings of the public."[21] Indeed, many pundits believed Munroe Sr. was on a fool's errand.

Governor General Young put little stock in newspaper rhetoric and even less in the ranting of a condemned man's father. He had already received a copy of the trial transcript as well as the opinions of his legal advisers. He would heed their counsel.[22] After Munroe spoke his piece, the governor general thanked him for his efforts, taking up the pages on offer. He then promised to give the matter his undivided attention, though he stopped short of making any actual commitments. Having reached the limits of his patience, Young plastered on a cherub's smile as he showed his supplicant the door.

John Munroe Sr. left elated. He told a band of waiting reporters that the meeting was successful. It was the futile boast of a man who'd lost control of his own destiny as well as that of his son. There was nothing more either Munroe could do now but wait and pray for mercy from the Crown.

Governor General Young made his ruling four days later—a deliberation long enough to indicate he had given the matter serious thought but too brief to engender any false hope. On January 25, 1870, Young signed order-in-council PC 1064 approving the execution of John A. Munroe. The architect would hang as scheduled on February 15. There were no more avenues of appeal and no possibility of an eleventh-hour stay of execution. John Munroe would swing and no one, save for Queen Victoria herself, could stop it.

TWENTY-FIVE

Given Enough Rope

In the days leading up to his execution, John Munroe became a wounded animal whose behaviour could no longer be predicted. He was kept in a debtor's cell, the nicest accommodations the jail offered, although nice was a relative concept. "He took little food," developed a leukemic pallor, and seemed "crushed" by his dramatic change in circumstance. The sheriff was sympathetic to Munroe's plight and, cognizant of his prisoner's social standing, granted him free access to friends and family. That few came to visit suited him, for he found the presence of others draining. Munroe's fettle and mettle continued to deteriorate as February 15 approached. He left his meals untouched, forsook his morning ablutions, and went hours without speaking. Days passed in which the architect did little more than stare at the wall.[1]

On February 10, Munroe's disposition took a marked turn for the better. He became livelier and engaged and his appetite returned in full force. The sheriff grew suspicious as Munroe grew increasingly verbose, at times almost charming. Guards were instructed to eavesdrop on his conversations. Their intelligence, coupled with a search of his cell, revealed an escape plan in the making. The scheme was simplicity itself: a distraction of the guard followed by a sprint through the cellblock door. The prisoner had no weapon or any means to procure one; he would be shielded only by his status and the element of surprise. The plan was thwarted, and Munroe was told he would be shot if he elected to run.

From that moment on, his guards were changed every four hours and visitor access was sharply restricted. On the rare occasions guests were permitted, a guard remained in the room at all times. Journalists were no longer welcome; their banishment resulted in some rather vague reporting. For instance, the final jailhouse visit by Munroe's father and brother was captured in rough silhouette: "It was doubtless a mournful spectacle, and one over which we gladly draw a veil."[2]

A state-sanctioned execution has all the spontaneity of a real estate closing. Killing a man in the name of God, Queen, and country required all courthouse totems to be erected as prescribed. Topping the list of empty rituals was the customary (some might say mandatory) meeting between the prisoner and the clergy. A common criminal typically received a token appearance by a single evangelist, but a man of Munroe's stature and celebrity warranted three men of the cloth. On February 14, 1870, as the clock's hour hand worked its way from nine until just past midnight, John Munroe welcomed the Reverends Stewart, Narraway, and Lathern, although Stewart did most of the talking.[3]

Having attended to the prisoner's soul, there remained the troublesome issue of its earthly vessel. The gallows were hastily constructed; built to finish what the courts had started. The resulting structure bent far from true and was mounted on knock-kneed struts that listed precariously. It was erected at the end of the building, near the jail's newly completed wing on Sydney Street.[4] The hanging apparatus was not the standard "long drop" noose, which uses the weight of the falling man to break his own neck. Rather, it relied on a system of lead weights that propelled the prisoner upward. The convoluted arrangement required iron counter-weights exceeding five hundred pounds to be raised into position by pulley and tackle.[5]

Here history takes an ironic pause, for legend has it that one of Munroe's earliest duties during his renovation of the jail was to design and construct the facility's new gallows. Allegedly he even created the counterweight system that would deliver him to the hereafter.[6] If true, Munroe would, quite literally, be hoisted by his own petard.

The ever-vain Munroe was determined to meet his maker looking his best, although his efforts fell short. His hair circled his head like a cloud, untamed by the pomades of the day. His once-immaculate facial hair grew wild, a patchwork field of mistimed crops. He wore black pants without braces, a white shirt, and leather boots. It was a workman's outfit, something he would never be caught dead in but was now fated to wear for eternity.[7]

John Munroe was scheduled to drop at eight o'clock on the morning of February 15. At 7:05 a.m., officials and spectators began to assemble in the jail's courtyard. There were the usual attendants: the sheriffs of Saint John, York, Westmorland, and Kings Counties; Constable Hankin; the coroner, Sylvester Earle, and his jury; and the three clergymen.[8] The city's mayor, some local magistrates, a few assorted medical professionals, and selected members of the press were also allotted viewing rights. The sheriff issued lottery tickets for the remaining spaces; the lucky recipients would be "admitted up till 7:30 am."[9] The ticket draw was tasteless, although scalpers made a pretty penny.

When the appointed hour approached, the assembled witnesses sang "Rock of Ages" as they moved toward the gallows. The hymn was accompanied by the pealing of church bells intended "to frighten timid and nervous women,"[10] discouraging them from joining the spectators. The bells failed miserably, for a group of women — "mostly apple vendors"[11] — gathered outside the jail as "rain poured down and the scene was perhaps the most uncomfortable that can be conceived."[12] The foul weather deterred a few, but hundreds were drawn by the irresistible urge of those low in the pecking order to prick at those lower still. Gawkers filled the courtyard and perched on the rooftops of houses that faced the jail. Several enterprising residents charged admission for prime viewing spots. One roof collapsed from the stress of so many spectators, and "a dull thump was heard from the street as the weight fell."[13]

The town square clock struck eight as the prisoner appeared. A hush fell over the crowd. John A. Munroe walked to the hanging tree "with a firm step."[14] An architect to the bitter end, he "looked up at the fatal beam, apparently to see that all was in order."[15] Before his arms were pinioned, he removed his gold watch and chain, the same one to which Maggie had once so brazenly affixed her image. He requested the items be given to his wife and sons.[16] Munroe paused to thank the sheriff for all the kindnesses extended to him, saying he hoped his death would serve as a warning to other men not to stray. Munroe's last words were recorded for posterity: "I hope you will all see me in heaven."[17]

The hangman stepped forward, placing a white cap over the condemned man's head. It partially obscured his face, coming to rest on the bridge of his nose. The noose was then secured. At a predetermined signal, the guide ropes holding the lead weights were cut. As the counterweights crashed down, "the miserable man was jerked from *terra firma*."[18] His body swayed, "then the hands began to work, the fingers clutching and then closing with a grip. The legs were not drawn up but by muscular contraction were turned over across the other somewhat. The neck was evidently not broken, death resulting from strangulation."[19] The reporter for the *Saint John Globe* saw "no evidence of pain, although the heart pulsated for a full twenty minutes."[20] His rival at the *Daily Morning News* seemed to be watching a different execution, for he was convinced Munroe "struggled hard, and his sufferings appeared to be terrible."[21] For twenty-five agonizing minutes, John Munroe dangled from a contraption of his own design. The body was cut down at the behest of the prison physician, Dr. Baxter.

Sylvester Earle ordered the body laid out in the tool shed. There, he held an inquest into the death of John Munroe. He called Constable Lewis Durant to confirm the identity of the deceased before conducting a brief autopsy. Earle and his jury, headed by foreman Christopher Armstrong, signed a declaration stating the sentence had been carried out and the prisoner was dead.

The final official act was to hoist a black flag, a sign to those outside the walls that the deed was done. As the flag unfurled, the chilled crowd cheered and then dispersed, leaving behind crumpled vestiges of their night. Be it carnival or execution, the detritus looks the same.

Munroe's body was placed in a simple black coffin. A silver plate engraved with his name and age was fixed to its lid. The casket was given to Constable Powers, who placed it on a sleigh. It sat there for more than eight hours while the constable and the surviving Munroes waited for the cover of darkness to transport the coffin to Fernhill Cemetery. Fernhill catered solely to the city's well heeled; John Munroe Sr. had purchased a premium plot in advance. The burial began immediately after the sledge arrived at the cemetery. It was over quickly. Bylaws prohibited any funeral ceremony, although the Reverends Stewart and Lathern each read short prayers. In a show of familial devotion, father John and brother George opened the coffin and kissed the corpse on the head before standing silently as the casket was closed and lowered into the grave.[22] It was the only public display of affection the family had ever shown.

Before John Munroe was even in the ground, bizarre rumours began to circulate. One account claimed the architect's neck was not broken by the hanging because he had hidden a protective brace under his high celluloid collar to prevent his neck from being permanently disfigured.[23] The tale was ludicrous but believable because it was in keeping with the condemned man's fastidious nature.

The *Daily Morning News* waxed maudlin when it noted, "From his very scaffold...his last glance might rest upon many fine edifices designed by his pencil and erected under his superintendence."[24] The fourth estate also found prescient symbolism in the oddest places: "Afterwards, it was noticed that the houses he had built were often decorated with wood carved to resemble rope."[25] The *Saint John Globe* left the purple prose to its competitors, choosing instead to transform Munroe's execution into a referendum on adultery: "The events of to-day would make all hearts humble. Who is so strong that he may not yield to temptation?" The editor tallied the wages of sin for a man unable to resist such wanton provocation: "It was a double murder, one the victim of his lustful passions, the other the offspring of that passion, an innocent babe."[26] In a widely read compendium printed moments after the fatal drop, editor George Day infused his précis with moral outrage. "We drop a tear over the deep depravity of human nature," wrote Day, "while we can scarce refrain from anathamatizing [*sic*] the memory of the man who left such an indelible stain upon the page of our country's history. Oh! may Munroe's ignominious death [serve] as a warning to seekers of illicit pleasure and other degrading vices."[27]

The Munroe family misfortunes did not end with the execution. The spring of 1895 saw three deaths in a clan bound by blood and shame. The first came on March 18, when his brother George died suddenly of pneumonia, having refused to summon a doctor.[28] Mary Eleanor Munroe passed quietly on May 16, and her husband John Jones Munroe followed just two days later, succumbing after a prolonged battle with bladder cancer.[29]

The era's rules of etiquette did not permit the execution of his favoured son to be mentioned in John J. Munroe's obituary. Euphemism alone marked that dark chapter: "Mr. Munroe had more than his share of troubles, but his resolution of strength and character carried him through troubles that would have killed many a man."[30]

TWENTY-SIX

Malum in Se

Throughout his ordeal, John A. Munroe seldom spoke publicly, but he had the last word after his death. A confession surfaced, purportedly written and signed by the architect and witnessed by clergymen Charles Stewart and John Lathern. It was shown to reporters immediately after the execution.

On their first trip to Black River Road, Munroe wrote, he and Maggie engaged in a little target practice — "she using the pistol I had given her," while he fired "a breach-loader" which he later "gave to a friend." The weather was pleasant, and "there was no intention on my part to harm her at that time."[1]

Two days later, Munroe was sharing a meal with his wife Annie during a visit to Fredericton when it occurred to him the copse of trees on Black River Road "was a suitable spot to commit a bad act." Upon his return to Saint John, Munroe escorted Maggie and Ella to the chosen location. While she settled the child on the large rock, he went into the bushes to steady his nerves. Just then, Ella began to cry. The sound enraged Munroe, who wrote: "I strangled the child. I do not know that it was actually dead." As Maggie fought to save Ella, Munroe coolly pulled a pistol from his pocket and shot her in the head. She fell to the ground. "A wallet with only a few dollars in it" tumbled from her skirt. Munroe took the cash, cast aside the wallet, covered the bodies with some hastily cut branches, "and left at once."[2]

Munroe also admitted taking some of the money from the sale of the Vails' house, "perhaps half or a little more." As for his motive, even he could not state why he did it. He had many reasons or none, depending on his mood: "I cannot say that money was not one of the motives for the act committed. I do not say it was in self-defence.... It was the money, my anger with her at the time, and my bad thoughts on and after the trip to Fredericton working together [that] caused me to do the bad act." Munroe also confessed he had written the letter to Phileanor Crear and asked a friend to mail it from Boston.[3]

Every newspaper on the eastern seaboard printed the confession in its entirety and then parsed it mercilessly. The *Saint John Globe* could not reconcile Munroe's eleventh hour *mea culpa* with his previous persona. "Indeed, the confession is so cold and, in a measure, so exculpatory, that we scarcely know what to make of it," the paper observed. "It is not apparently the work of a man who has thoroughly realized the appalling nature of the crime committed, or aroused to a full sense of the wrong he had done to the moral law which he had outraged."[4] The point was well taken, for his declaration contained not a whiff of remorse.

As if to prove the point, Munroe ended his confession with a curious proclamation: "I never killed any other person or child."[5] Sometimes it is the sins you do not commit that are your only saving grace.

The startling thing about evil in this world is not that it exists, but that no one expects it. Malevolence percolates in the most unlikely places, perpetrated by those of otherwise exemplary character. The law recognizes the concept of *malum in se* (evil in itself) declaring crimes such as murder to be "inherently immoral."[6] Yet the law also separates the components of the crime. The act may be evil, but the actor is not.

The Victorians drew cold comfort from their certainty that men like John Munroe were congenitally good. In the decades since, we have abandoned much (though not all) of our class-based prejudices regarding crime, yet we still confuse morality with criminality. Our theories on crime and those who commit it have evolved, but our beliefs have not necessarily kept pace.

There was a time in our legal history when all evidence was created equal, when our ability to interpret physical, testimonial, and character evidence was on level footing. By going back in time and examining the case against John Munroe with fresh eyes, we see what has changed and what has stayed the same. In the nearly 150 years since Munroe defended his good name, forensic science has been defined as a discipline, and its techniques and methodologies have developed at an extraordinary rate. Tectonic shifts have also occurred in how the courts deal with witness testimony. Accused persons can now speak in their own defence, and the admission of hearsay has been sharply curtailed. The notion of character as evidence, however, remains the same. The legal system has grown up around the issue of character, leaving it stunted and inchoate by comparison.

There is always a danger in looking back, as the past can seem simplistic or even quaint by modern standards. Yet it is the very naivety of Munroe and his crime that makes this case so informative and relevant to today's legal system. John Munroe lived in a time before popular culture transformed murder into entertainment. In the days before televised forensic procedurals, courtroom dramas, or even Sherlock Holmes,[7] Munroe was blithely unaware of police procedure or investigative techniques. He had not learned how to get away with murder. Today's audience, reared on a steady diet of crime, is much savvier. No doubt you easily identified ways in which Munroe could have covered his tracks: using different cab drivers, perhaps, or purchasing the murder weapon in Boston where it could not be traced. Munroe's efforts were clumsy but they clearly revealed his intent. More than a century on, we can see a man make a decision, then act on it. The simplicity of the case allows us to separate the signal from the noise.

The theory of universal lethality holds that to kill is a decision. That decision is either made in the moment (a crime of passion or second-degree murder) or — as in the case of John Munroe — with forethought and planning (premeditated or first-degree murder). It is also a decision like any other—whether to marry, quit a job, or rob a bank—reached through the same deliberative process. In debating the pros and cons of murder, there are no universal standards. Those with strong religious beliefs may put great stock in the concepts of heaven or hell, but such constructs do not factor into the decisions of atheists, agnostics, or those embracing alternative spirituality. By the same token, incarceration or the death penalty are not deterrents for those convinced they will never be caught. There is also no universal morality. The taking of a human life is not always considered wrong: war, capital punishment, self-defence, abortion, assisted suicide. We do not all draw the line in the same place. If you are ever called for jury duty, the law requires you to be clear about what you are condemning. The accused's values do not need to align with yours, and it is not a crime for the defendant to have weighed the risks and rewards differently than you might.

Murder as a decision-making process brings us to the question of motive. Here, definitions are crucial. While motive is the personal justification for the act, intent is the mental resolve to commit it. Unlike math students, those accused of murder do not need to show their work. The law recognizes murder as *malum in se*, evil in itself; therefore, there are no "good" reasons to commit it. Unfortunately, when it comes to motive, pop culture once again rears its ugly head. Fictitious depictions of court proceedings reinforce the erroneous notion that motive is central in every murder trial, yet nothing could be further from reality. Set aside what you have gleaned from pop culture and go back to the law itself. The statutes clearly state: "When the intent to do an act that violates the law exists, motive becomes immaterial."[8] Legally it does not matter whether John killed Maggie because of the money, or because she was pregnant, or because he simply grew tired of her. It is his actions that violate the law, not his character or his values.

And therein lies the fatal flaw in universal lethality. The theory is only good in theory; it falters in application because of human nature. We want to know why John Munroe killed Maggie Vail and Ella Munroe. Juries will not convict if the prosecution does not provide a motive, even though the law only requires evidence of intent, not motivation. Jurors often struggle with the theory of universal lethality for the same reason they ignore the law when it comes to motive: it just feels wrong.

The absence of motive is not the only reason many are uncomfortable with universal lethality theory. If everyone is capable of murder, what does that say about you and the people you love? We use labels to distance ourselves from murderers: they are evil, crazy, psychopathic, sociopathic, or narcissistic. Perhaps your own initial instinct was to diagnose Munroe, and you are not alone in that impulse. Still, the link between psychopathy and murder is based on a false syllogism. Not all psychopaths commit murder, and not all murderers are psychopaths. The only equation that matters is psychopathy = motivation = legally irrelevant. Universal lethality theory requires no such labels.[9] The prosecutor need prove only that the accused committed the act, not that there was something "wrong" with him. This should simplify matters, but it does not, because the theory implies murder is a club anyone can join. That thought makes us uneasy.

Has the time come for us to formally remove the issue of character from criminal trials? The courts have tried to vanquish character evidence: the law does not recognize character as a necessary element of the crime and motive is deemed immaterial. Science has also done what it can to temper the effects of character, postulating theories that render it irrelevant. Yet the accused's moral turpitude continues to dominate criminal proceedings, an endless source of bias, misdirection, and emotional bearbaiting. Despite advances in forensic science and legal procedure, the issue of character remains immune to objective scrutiny and testing. We still rely on our guts to make life and death assessments.

Our system of jurisprudence is a reflection of the people it serves. We the people persist in dragging the issue of character into a court of law, and only we the people can remove it.

ACKNOWLEDGEMENTS

To shamelessly crib Hillary Rodham Clinton, it takes a village to write a book like this. I am forever indebted to Joanna Alton Kerr, archivist, and Jane Anne Wilson and Julia Thompson, photograph archivists, at the Provincial Archives of New Brunswick, for their ceaseless efforts to find materials associated with this case. Thanks also to Alexandra McEwen and her fellow archivists at the National Library and Archive in Ottawa for their efforts. A tip of the hat to Barb at Fernhill Cemetery in Saint John for forwarding a slew of Munroe burial records. Dr. Leah Grandy, microforms assistant at the Harriet Irving Library at the University of New Brunswick, also provided a much-needed hand. As always, I am grateful to my literary agent, Carolyn Swayze, for her efforts in getting my books to market.

I also offer my sincere thanks to former New Mexico governor Bill Richardson, former chief medical examiner Dr. Ross Zumwalt, and the notorious outlaw Billy the Kid. This motley assemblage played a key role in the most ludicrous episode of my professional career: the 2004 criminal inquiry into the death of Billy the Kid. It was a silly and wasteful endeavour (and a true abuse of taxpayer dollars), but it was the genesis of where I am now. For that, I am eternally grateful.

Finally, I owe everything to the wonderful people at Goose Lane Editions— Susanne Alexander, Martin Ainsley, Julie Scriver, Chris Tompkins, Colleen Kitts, Kathleen Peacock, Angela Williams, and all the staff—for giving me a safe and supportive place to learn and grow as a writer. Thanks also to my editor, Sarah Brohman, who makes me crazy and a better writer in equal measure, and to Paula Sarson for her tireless efforts in proofreading.

NOTES

All references to witness testimony drawn from the coroner's inquest, the police magistrate examination, and the trial transcripts are from the master case file Crown v. Munro [*sic*] housed at the Library and Archives Canada, RG 13, volume 1408, file 23A.

A redacted compendium of the transcripts edited by George W. Day, "The Black River Road Tragedy: Full Reports of the Coroner's Inquest and the Trial of John A. Munroe for the Murder of Sarah Margaret Vail and Ella May Munroe," 1869, is available at the New Brunswick Museum Archives, UNC SVEC 346.4 B627, hereafter referred to as Day's compendium.

PREFACE THE DAHMER EFFECT

1. Details of Dahmer's crimes drawn from Donald A. Davis, *The Jeffrey Dahmer Story: An American Nightmare* (New York: St. Martin's Press, 1991); and Michael Newton, *The Encyclopedia of Serial Killers*, 2nd ed. (New York: Checkmark Books, 2006).

2. Dale Keiger, "The Dark World of Park Dietz," *Johns Hopkins Magazine* (November 1994), accessed June 23, 2014, http://www.jhu.edu/jhumag/1194web/dietz.html.

3. Dietz explained his theory in detail in Willis Spaulding, "Park Dietz: The Killing Expert Who Knows Too Much," *The Hook* 248 (December 2003): 22-31. While most in the forensic community embrace the notion that murder is a decision everyone is capable of, many challenge Dietz's contention that everyone "will" kill. The capacity to kill is universal, but murder is not necessarily inevitable or mandatory.

4. Ibid., 25.

5. Ludwig Wittgenstein, *Tractatus Logico-Philosphicus* (1922; repr., Oxford: Routledge, 2014), xxi.

6. Christopher Grivas and Debra Komar, "Kumho, Daubert and the Nature of Scientific Inquiry: Implications for Forensic Anthropology," *Journal of Forensic Sciences* 53, no. 4 (2008): 771-76.

PROLOGUE ABERRANT, ABHORRENT VAPOURS

1. Biographic details from George Cunningham, trial testimony, December 10, 1869.

2. Elizabeth Cunningham, trial testimony, December 14, 1869.

3. George Cunningham, trial testimony, December 10, 1869.

4. George Parker, trial testimony, December 11, 1869.

5. Fingerboards were precursors to today's roadside mileage signs, posted at intersections to direct travellers.

6. Robert Holmes, trial testimony, December 13, 1869.

7. *St. John Daily Telegraph and Morning Journal*, September 18, 1869.

ONE SAINT JOHN

1. John's birthdate and the details of Munroe's parents' wedding were printed in the *New Brunswick Courier*, May 30, 1840.

2. Although no birth registrations can be found for the four infants who died, their births and deaths were recorded on the monument marking the Munroe family plot in Fernhill Cemetery, as well as in the facility's burial records. See, for example, the Fernhill Cemetery's official website, www.fernhill cemetery.ca/fernhill/. Records relating to the Munroe family are contained in the Fernhill Cemetery perpetual care record book, lots 698 and 796.

3. Alice Munroe's registry of live birth, Provincial Archives of New Brunswick [PANB], RS141A 1b, 1861-M-77, F18758, registration number 19755.

4. The Sydney Street firehouse is now a museum and national historic site, www.historicplaces.ca/en/rep-reg/place-lieu.aspx?id=13472&pid=0. The website details the role John Cunningham played in the building's design and construction.

5. For his role as a founding member of Centenary Methodist Church, see John Munroe Sr.'s obituary in the *St. John Daily Telegraph and Morning Journal*, May 20, 1895.

6. J.R. Marshall, trial testimony, December 11, 1869.

7. Gary K. Hughes, *Music of the Eye: Architectural Drawings of Canada's First City, 1822 to 1914* (Saint John: New Brunswick Museum and the Royal Architecture Institute of Canada, 1992).

8. J.R. Marshall, a lifelong friend and neighbour of Munroe's, noted during his trial testimony on December 11, 1869, that he had never known the man to leave the city for any length of time.

9. The fates of the Munroe daughters derived from their father's obituary in the *St. John Daily Telegraph and Morning Journal*, May 20, 1895. Robert Craig's profession was noted on the birth registry of his daughter, Mary Elizabeth Craig, PANB RS141A1b, 1880-C-105, F18767. It is worth noting, however, that Fernhill Cemetery records indicate Alice Munroe was unmarried upon her death in 1948. A letter sent to the cemetery by Alice in 1940 (retained in the Fernhill records) lists her address as Seattle, and she identifies herself as "Miss Munroe." She left New Brunswick for Seattle, ostensibly to marry a man named Wilmot, but whether the marriage actually occurred cannot be confirmed.

10. One local history claims that "after finishing school young John went to work in the office of his father's lumberyard," but provides no sources to support this contention. The declaration seems suspect, for by that time John's school days were well behind him and his career as an architect was in full swing. Peter Little, "The Sad Tale of Maggie Vail," *The New Brunswick Reader*, n.d., accessed May 20, 2013, http://new-brunswick.net/new-brunswick/ghoststory/ghost2.html.

11. John Munroe Sr. bragged of his son's success during his trial testimony on December 14, 1869, as well as to countless reporters covering the trial.

12. Munroe's design of the asylum is documented in the McCord Museum Collection, accession number X11891. Additional design credits can be found in Charles D. Grant, "History of Cleasby House," *Kings County Record*, 1980, accessed February 13, 2013, http://rothesaylivingmuseum.nbed.nb.ca/RAHeritageTrust/raht-hcorner/cleasby.html.

13. The sequential destruction of specific buildings is detailed in George Stewart Jr., *The Story of the Great Fire in St. John N.B., June 20, 1877.* (Saint John, NB: Belford Brothers, 1877).

14. Newspaper reportage in the Victorian era was curiously fashion fixated, even when it came to criminal trials. Every paper's coverage of daily events included a summary of the key players' wardrobes (complete with commentary by the reporter). See, for example, *Daily Morning News*, September 22, 1869.

During her inquest testimony of September 30, Phileanor Crear described Munroe as "vain" and presenting a "false, inflated" persona.

15. John Munroe's appearance is evident in the surviving images of him (drawings and photographs printed in the newspapers), most notably in the ever-changing length of his whiskers during the trial as he struggled to keep abreast of the latest trends.

16. Their marriage certificate is retained at the PANB, F9093, 1862, #857.

17. William Belding, trial testimony, December 15, 1869.

TWO **LOW HANGING FRUIT**

1. Speculation as to the health of Munroe's marriage comes from the inquest and trial testimony of Maggie Vail's sister Phileanor Crear, an admittedly biased source. According to Crear, Munroe made countless comments to Maggie regarding his wife's cold and distant nature while they were courting. It also bears noting that Annie Munroe was not included in the list of character witnesses offered by Munroe's defence team during the trial. In fact, Annie Munroe never broke her silence regarding her husband's misdeeds for the remainder of her life.

2. Louisa Ells, trial testimony, December 9, 1869.

3. Edward Price, trial testimony, December 16, 1869.

4. Jacob Vail, trial testimony, December 10, 1869.

5. Details of Maggie Vail's appearance and teeth drawn from the coroner's inquest testimony of Sarah Lake and Jane McLaren on September 22, 1869, and that of Louisa Ells on September 24.

6. The abundance of fashion-related clippings contained within her trunk, which were inventoried during the coroner's inquest on October 2, 1869, demonstrates Maggie's reliance on women's journals.

7. Maggie Vail's character and her feelings regarding Munroe were discussed at length during the testimony of her sisters Phileanor Crear and Rebecca Olive at the coroner's inquest on September 30, 1869.

8. Maggie's relationship with her mother and the death of Mrs. Vail was recalled during the trial testimony of Jacob Vail on December 10, 1869.

9. The Vail family history was detailed during Phileanor Crear's inquest testimony on September 3, 1869, and her testimony at trial on December 13, 1869.

10. Phileanor Crear, trial testimony, December 13, 1869.

11. The first meeting of Maggie Vail and John Munroe was recounted in the witness statement of Phileanor Crear before the police magistrate on October 7, 1869.

12. Ibid.

13. Phileanor Crear, statement to police magistrate, October 7, 1869.

14. Ibid.

15. The specifics regarding their early courtship come from the testimony of Maggie's sisters during the inquest and trial.

16. Phileanor Crear, statement to police magistrate, October 7, 1869.

17. Phileanor Crear, trial testimony, December 13, 1869.

18. Ibid.

19. Phileanor Crear, statement to police magistrate, October 7, 1869.

20. Phileanor Crear, trial testimony, December 13, 1869.

21. Munroe's gifts were catalogued during Phileanor Crear's recall testimony at the inquest, October 2, 1869.

22. Phileanor Crear, inquest testimony, September 30, 1869.

23. The framed photograph was discussed at length during Phileanor Crear's appearance at the coroner's inquest on September 30, 1869. The actual photograph was admitted into evidence following the inventory of Maggie's trunk at the inquest on October 2, 1869.

24. The requests and exchange of reciprocal photographs were detailed during the trial when Phileanor Crear was recalled to the stand on December 13, 1869.

25. Phileanor Crear, inquest testimony, September 30, 1869.

26. Jacob Vail, inquest testimony, September 27, 1869.

27. Rebecca Olive, inquest testimony, September 30, 1869.

28. *Daily Morning News*, September 30, 1869.

29. Phileanor Crear, statement to police magistrate, October 7, 1869.

THREE **HOLLOW THREATS AND LOADED QUESTIONS**

1. Phileanor Crear, trial testimony, December 13, 1869.

2. Phileanor Crear, statement to police magistrate, October 7, 1869.

3. Phileanor Crear, trial testimony, December 13, 1869.

4. Phileanor Crear, statement to police magistrate, October 7, 1869.

5. Ibid.

6. Details of Ella's birth taken from the inquest testimony of Dr. M.H. Peters on September 22, 1869, as well as that of Phileanor Crear on September 30.

7. Dr. M.H. Peters, inquest testimony, September 22, 1869.

8. Phileanor Crear, inquest testimony, September 30, 1869.

9. Phileanor Crear, statement to police magistrate, October 7, 1869.

10. Phileanor Crear, statement to police magistrate on October 7, 1869, and her subsequent trial testimony.

11. James Olive's biographical details taken from the 1851 Census as well as his testimony at the coroner's inquest on September 22, 1869.

12. Vail's estate is described in the St. John County probate records for 1785-1912, PANB, RS 71.

13. Phileanor Crear, trial testimony, December 13, 1869. Crear claimed to have overheard Munroe coerce Maggie into selling the house.

14. John C. Littlehale, trial testimony, December 9, 1869.

15. James Olive, inquest testimony, September 22, 1869. At that time, each bank produced its own paper currency. Money changes hands several times throughout the remainder of the story, yet investigators never bothered to check whether those bills were from the Commercial or St. Stephen's bank — one of many valuable evidentiary avenues not followed.

16. James Olive, inquest testimony, September 22, 1869. Phileanor Crear also recounted the sale of the house during her inquest testimony on September 30, although she claimed Maggie had $575 placed in her bosom.

17. John C. Littlehale, trial testimony, December 9, 1869.

FOUR SHIP OF FOOLS

1. Phileanor Crear, inquest testimony, September 30, 1869.

2. As John Munroe was not permitted to testify in his own defence, Captain Francis Jones entered into evidence a summary of Munroe's witness statement before the police magistrate on October 2, 1869, during the coroner's inquest.

3. The coroner, Sylvester Earle, summarized Munroe's trip as part of his own trial testimony on December 14, 1869.

4. Munroe recounted their conversation during his statement to the police magistrate; recounted by Francis Jones, inquest testimony, October 2, 1869.

5. Ibid.

6. Ibid.

7. Accounts differ as to Munroe's movements. The coroner later testified at trial (on December 14) to an alternate timeline from the one presented by Captain Jones. In both accounts, however, the sequence of events remained the same.

8. From Munroe's statement to the police magistrate; recounted by Francis Jones, inquest testimony, October 2, 1869.

9. Munroe's employment with Clarke was mentioned in Phileanor Crear's inquest testimony on September 30, 1869.

10. Francis Jones, inquest testimony, October 2, 1869; Munroe, Jones recounted, said he "did not see her but once on deck till they got to St. John."

11. The attorney general referred to Maggie as a whore and a strumpet during his closing arguments, December 16, 1869.

12. Mary Ann Lordly, inquest testimony, September 22, 1869; Robert Worden, trial testimony, December 8, 1869.

13. Mary Ann Lordly, inquest testimony, September 22, 1869.

14. Ibid.

15. Ibid.

16. Ibid.

17. The fees for room and board were reported in *Daily Morning News*, September 22, 1869.

18. Mary Ann Lordly, inquest testimony, September 22, 1869.

FIVE IN SIN AND ERROR PINING

1. The entire trip was discussed at length during the coroner's inquest testimony of Robert Worden on September 20, 1869, and again during his trial testimony on December 8, 1869.

2. Robert Worden, inquest testimony, September 20, 1869.

3. Robert Worden, trial testimony, December 8, 1869.

4. Robert Worden, inquest testimony, September 20, 1869.

5. George Bunker, trial testimony, December 9, 1869.

6. Robert Worden, inquest testimony, September 20, 1869.

7. Ibid.

8. Maggie's side of the story comes from the testimony of Phileanor Crear at the inquest and the trial, as well as from the landlady of the hotel.

9. To the coroner, Munroe described Maggie's mood that morning as jovial and light. According to Munroe, they did not quarrel and she remained in good spirits throughout the journey.

10. Several members of the Collins family as well as everyone else who lived on the road testified at the trial that Munroe and Maggie made no effort to visit the Collins home.

11. William Lake, inquest testimony, September 20, 1869.

12. Sarah Lake, inquest testimony, September 20, 1869.

13. Ibid.

14. Thorne biography and the purchase of Burpee's Ironworks in 1870 drawn from "Candidates of Mayoralty," *Saint John Globe*, April 9, 1887; the entry for Henry J. Thorne from the "Loyalist Families Genealogy of United Empire Loyalists in New Brunswick Canada," http://loyalistfamilies.com/henry-thorne-and-family/ and supported by Isaac Burpee's estate papers, New Brunswick Museum Archives, S110 112, F3 18.

15. Robert Robertson, trial testimony, December 10, 1869.

16. Robert Robertson, inquest testimony, September 27, 1869.

17. Ibid.

SIX **FORCED PERSPECTIVE**

1. Although no official meteorological data exists for October 31, 1868, Gilbert Murdock, the superintendent of sewage and water supply for the county, "kept quite an extensive record" of the region's weather and testified at trial on December 15, 1869.

2. Robert Worden, inquest testimony, September 20, 1869; trial testimony, December 8, 1869.

3. Robert Worden, trial testimony, December 8, 1869.

4. George Bunker, trial testimony, December 9, 1869.

5. Robert Worden, trial testimony, December 8, 1869.

6. George Bunker, trial testimony, December 9, 1869.

7. Robert Worden's trial testimony, December 8, 1869.

8. Ibid.

9. George Bunker, trial testimony, December 9, 1869.

10. Robert Worden, trial testimony, December 8, 1869.

11. Ibid.

12. John Munroe, statement to police magistrate, September 21, 1869.

13. Phileanor Crear, inquest testimony, September 30, 1869.

14. *Daily Morning News*, September 30, 1869.

15. Phileanor Crear, inquest testimony, September 30, 1869.

16. Ibid.

17. Philly Crear first mentioned the letter during her inquest testimony on September 30. The letter and envelope were admitted into evidence by the coroner that same day.

18. The letter was read into evidence at the inquest on September 30, 1869. The spelling and punctuation reproduced here are from Ruby M. Cusack's *Yesteryear: The Maggie Vail Story* (Saint John, NB: printed by author, 1987), available in special collections at the Saint John Free Public Library.

19. Phileanor Crear, inquest testimony, September 30, 1869.

SEVEN **INTO THE WOODS**

1. Arthur Bousfield and Gary Toffoli, *Home to Canada: Royal Tours 1786-2010* (Tonawanda, ON: Dundurn Press, 2010).

2. *Daily Morning News*, September 17, 1869.

3. Martha Thompson, inquest testimony, September 16, 1869.

4. The discovery of the remains was recounted in Martha's inquest testimony, as well as that of Caroline and Margaret Thompson, George Diggs, and Henry Brandy, September 16, 1869.

5. The females' version of events was taken from the inquest testimony of Martha Thompson, Susan Lane, and Margaret Thompson, September 16, 1869. For the males' account, see the testimony of Henry Brandy and George Diggs on the same day.

6. Caroline Thompson, inquest testimony, September 16, 1869.

7. Susan Lane, inquest testimony, September 16, 1869.

8. William Douglas gave identical accounts of the exchange when he testified at the inquest on September 16 and at the trial on December 8, 1869.

9. William Douglas, inquest testimony, September 16, 1869.

10. William Douglas, trial testimony, December 8, 1869.

11. Ibid.

12. *St. John Daily Telegraph and Morning Journal*, September 17, 1869; William Douglas, trial testimony on December 8, 1869.

13. *Daily Morning News*, September 17, 1869.

14. *St. John Daily Telegraph and Morning Journal*, September 17, 1869.

15. *St. John Daily Telegraph and Morning Journal*, September 20, 1869.

16. Horace Bunker, inquest testimony, September 23, 1869.

17. *St. John Daily Telegraph and Morning Journal*, September 20, 1869.

18. Ibid.

EIGHT **ASHES AND DUST**

1. Sylvester Zobieski Earle entry in the *Dictionary of Canadian Biography Online*, accessed March 28, 2013, www.biographi.ca/009004-119.01-e.php?BioId= 39622&query=.

2. Typically, dead houses were the dissection rooms associated with medical schools. The city's dead house was mentioned in James Christie's inquest testimony, September, 28, 1869.

3. *Hutchinson's Directory*, 1867-1868; *Lovell's Directory*, 1871.

4. James Christie, trial testimony, December 11, 1869.

5. James Christie, inquest testimony, September 28, 1869, and trial testimony, December 11, 1869.

6. LeBaron Botsford, trial testimony, December 11, 1869.

7. James Christie, inquest testimony, September 28, 1869. Like the ubiquitous but erroneous urban legend regarding the number of Inuit words for snow, the lead fragments lining a gunshot wound have since been buried under a flurry of forensic scientific jargon. Terms include "wipe" (D.A. Komar and J.E. Buikstra, *Forensic Anthropology: Contemporary Theory and Practice* [New York: Oxford University Press, 2008], 179); "metallic snow" (Werner U. Spitz, ed., *Spitz and Fisher's Medicolegal Investigation of Death: Guidelines for the Application of Pathology to Crime Investigation*, 4th ed. [Springfield, IL: Charles C. Thomas, 2006], 664); or a "lead snowstorm" (V.J.M. Di Maio, *Gunshot Wounds: Practical Aspects of Firearms, Ballistics, and Forensic Techniques*, 2nd ed. [Boca Raton: CRC Press, 1999], 318).

8. James Christie, inquest testimony, September 28, 1869.

9. Christie used the term "meningen" in his inquest testimony on September 28, 1869, and again at the trial on December 11, 1869. The "meningen" artery is currently correctly referred to as the anterior branch of the middle meningeal artery. See, for example, Anne M.R. Agur, *Grant's Atlas of Anatomy*, 9th ed. (Baltimore: Williams and Wilkins, 1991).

10. James Christie, inquest testimony, September 28, 1869.

11. Ibid.

12. Ibid.

13. *St. John Daily Telegraph and Morning Journal*, September 20, 1869.

14. James Christie, trial testimony, December 11, 1869. Tooth wear (dental attrition) was commonly used to determine age for much of the twentieth century—see, for example, Douglas H. Ubelaker, *Human Skeletal Remains: Excavation, Analysis, Interpretation*, 2nd ed. (Taraxacum, WA: Manuals on Archeology 2, 1989), 91-92—but has fallen out of favour in recent decades because the method lacks precision. Bone softness (i.e., the degree of ossification) can be an effective means of aging subadult remains, but it is not a reliable indicator of age in full adults and requires radiographic assessment. See: Louise Scheuer and Sue Black, *Developmental Juvenile Osteology* (New York: Elsevier Academic Press, 2000).

15. James Christie, trial testimony, December 11, 1869. The method came to be known as Cranial Suture Closure Assessment and was widely used from the late 1800s through the late 1990s. See, for example, S.T. Brooks, "Skeletal Age at Death: Reliability of Cranial and Pubic Age Indicators," *American Journal of Physical Anthropology* 13 (1955): 567-97. The method is no longer accepted as it fails to meet the standards of modern forensic science.

16. James Christie, trial testimony, December 11, 1869, cited Botsford's private comments.

17. LeBaron Botsford, trial testimony, December 11, 1869.

18. James Christie, inquest testimony, September 28, 1869.

19. *St. John Daily Telegraph and Morning Journal*, September 20, 1869.

20. James Christie, trial testimony, December 11, 1869.

21. LeBaron Botsford, trial testimony, December 11, 1869.

22. *St. John Daily Telegraph and Morning Journal*, September 20, 1869.

23. George W. Day, ed. "The Black River Road Tragedy: Full Reports of the Coroner's Inquest and the Trial of John A. Munroe for the Murder of Sarah Margaret Vail and Ella May Munroe," (1869), 5 [hereafter cited as Day's compendium].

24. The names of the coroner's jury were noted in Earle's report of his inquest, as well as in Day's compendium and every newspaper that covered the inquest.

25. At this point in Canadian history, the powers of the coroner had been (very vaguely) codified in legal statutes, specifically relating to their authority to collect taxes for the Crown (the original job description of a coroner). Those powers included subpoena (the ability to compel testimony) and the right to seize property without a warrant. The rights and responsibilities of police, on the other hand, had not yet been formally set down in law. Many of the protections now afforded by law (such as the right to have an attorney present

during questions or the need to Mirandize prisoners — both exclusively American rights yet familiar to Canadians thanks to films and TV) were still decades in the future. In 1869 the role of the police was closer to that of social custodian — handling drunks and cattle at large — rather than investigation or law enforcement. The expansion and codification of police powers would not come until the following century. An informative history of the development of the coroner's system is Bernard Knight, "Crowner: Origins of the Office of Coroner," 2007, www.britannia.com/history/coroner1.html.

NINE RAISING CAIN

1. Richard Burke, "Introduction," *Indiantown: A Town Forgotten* (Saint John, NB: self-published, 1988).

2. The surname of the accused was variably reported as "Kane" (see, for example, Day's compendium [1869]); "Kain" (*Daily Morning News*, September 20, 1869); and "Cain" (*Daily Morning News*, September 21, 1869). Review of historical documents, including the census, local directories, and governmental records reveals the correct spelling is Cain, which is used here. *Hutchinson's Directory*, 1867; *Lovell's Directory*, 1871. See also Village Plan 3 (southwest) — Indiantown (town of Portland), in F.B. Roe and N. George Colby, *Atlas of Saint John City and County, New Brunswick, 1875* (Saint John, NB: Roe & Colby, 1875).

3. *Daily Morning News*, September 20, 1869.

4. The press reported Mary Cain's family squabbles at length, and her address was noted in *Hutchinson's Directory*, 1867.

5. Registry of Canadian Historic Places, accessed June 27, 2014, www.historicplaces.ca/en/rep-reg/place-lieu.aspx?id=11928.

6. *Daily Morning News*, September 21, 1869.

7. Although many people testified that Cain was legally married to the woman in Indiantown (for example, Mary Cain and Samuel Peters at the coroner's inquest on September 20, 1869), no record of his marriage survives in the records at the Provincial Archives of New Brunswick. Every newspaper covering the story mentions his wife but does not identify her by name, and no clues to her identity can be derived from any of the federated databases in the provincial archives.

8. Much of the tale of Cain and the "other woman" comes from the inquest testimony of Samuel Peters and Mary Cain, who took the stand on September 20, 1869.

9. James Sprague, inquest testimony, September 20, 1869.

10. Samuel Peters, inquest testimony, September 20, 1869.

11. George C. Dunham, inquest testimony, September 20, 1869.

12. James Sprague, inquest testimony, September 20, 1869.

13. Samuel Peters, inquest testimony, September 20, 1869.

14. Mary Cain, inquest testimony, September 20, 1869. Samuel Peters, George Dunham, and James Sprague acknowledged Mary Cain as the source of the rumours, but she denied saying any such thing during her testimony at the inquest.

15. *Daily Morning News*, September 20, 1869.

16. Sylvester Earle, statement to police magistrate, October 6, 1869. Earle's testimony quoted Worden's words.

17. *St. John Daily Telegraph and Morning Journal*, September 22, 1869. Police records (Library and Archives Canada, RG 13, volume 1408, file 23A) contain no warrant in George's name, and Dr. Earle's report and testimony make no mention of the mix-up. According to the coroner, John A. Munroe simply "called to see me during the investigation" and there was no mention of the mishap in Earle's testimony before the police magistrate, October 6, 1869, although that may just have been Earle covering his own mistake.

18. *St. John Daily Telegraph and Morning Journal*, September 22, 1869, and Samuel Thomson's closing remarks at trial, December 16, 1869.

19. That Thomson practised law from his home office is noted in *Hutchinson's Directory*, 1867.

20. *Daily Morning News*, September 22, 1869.

TEN **WHAT FRESH HELL**

1. Jemima Lane, inquest testimony, September 20, 1869. A case narrative differs from the general public's perception of a story, as gleaned from newspaper accounts. It contains only the facts of the case as established by stipulation, testimony, or physical evidence admitted at a hearing.

2. Jane Davidson, inquest testimony, September 20, 1869. The *Telegraph* lambasted her appearance. *St. John Daily Telegraph and Morning Journal*, September 21, 1869.

3. Although Samuel Peters identified himself as a raftsman during his inquest testimony on September 20, 1869, his listing in *Hutchinson's Directory*, 1865, notes his profession as lumber driver.

4. Samuel Peters, inquest testimony, September 20, 1869.

5. The correspondent's account ran later that same day. *Daily Morning News*, September 20, 1869.

6. Samuel Peters, inquest testimony, September 20, 1869.

7. Mary Cain's coarse appearance and personality were topics of much discussion among her neighbours, many of whom also testified on September 20, 1869. See, for example, the statements of James Sprague or George Dunham. James Cain, in his statement to the coroner, also had nothing kind to say about his aunt or her character.

8. Mary Cain, inquest testimony, September 20, 1869.

9. Ibid.

10. *Daily Morning News*, September 20, 1869; *Daily Morning News*, September 21, 1869.

11. George Dunham, inquest testimony, September 20, 1869.

12. James Williams, inquest testimony, September 20, 1869.

13. James Sprague, inquest testimony, September 20, 1869.

14. Day's compendium, 9.

15. Jeremiah Travis, *A Law Treatise on the Constitutional Powers of Parliament, and of the Local Legislatures, under the British North America Act, 1867* (Saint John, NB: self-published, 1884), np. Travis's dire assessment of Wetmore was echoed by T.W. Acheson in Wetmore's entry in the *Dictionary of Canadian Biography*, vol. 12, University of Toronto/Université Laval 2003, accessed March 16, 2016, http://www.biographi.ca/en/bio/wetmore_andrew_rainsford_12E.html.

16. Although Wetmore would later find himself on opposing legal sides with Munroe, he made his esteem for patricians in general and Munroe's social status in particular known during his opening and closing remarks at trial.

ELEVEN **FULL COOPERATION**

1. Records show that Earle was at the crime scene that day, but whom he was with varies. On September 22, 1869, the *St. John Daily Telegraph and Morning Journal* reported that Munroe was forced to wait because Earle was at the crime scene with Robert Worden, but this account is inconsistent with court records, which indicate the coroner was at the scene with his jury on that date.

2. Sylvester Earle, statement to police magistrate, October 6, 1869. Detainees in Canada still do not have the right to have a lawyer present during police interrogation. The Supreme Court reaffirmed this ruling as recently as 2010

in the case R. v. Sinclair. "No right to lawyer in police interview: top court," CBC, October 8, 2010, accessed May 6, 2013, www.cbc.ca/news/canada/ story/2010/10/08/supreme-court-charter-right-lawyer-interview.html.

3. Sylvester Earle, statement to police magistrate, October 6, 1869.

4. Sylvester Earle was not permitted to testify at his own inquest. As previously noted, Francis Jones entered into evidence some quotes attributed to Munroe on October 2, 1869. Earle later confirmed these quotes when he testified before the police magistrate on October 6, 1869.

5. Francis Jones, inquest testimony, October 2, 1869; Sylvester Earle, statement to police magistrate, October 6, 1869.

6. Sylvester Earle, statement to police magistrate, October 6, 1869.

7. Ibid.

8. Ibid.

9. Francis Jones, inquest testimony, October 2, 1869.

10. Ibid.

11. Sylvester Earle, statement to police magistrate, October 6, 1869.

12. Ibid.

13. Ibid.

14. *St. John Daily Telegraph and Morning Journal*, September 22, 1869. Earle was right to be cautious, as a coroner does not have the authority to make an arrest.

15. Sylvester Earle, statement to police magistrate, October 6, 1869.

TWELVE **HAMPERING AND TAMPERING**

1. The events described in this chapter were recounted during the inquest testimony of Francis Jones on October 2, 1869, and in Sylvester Earle's and Abram Craft's statements to the police magistrate on October 6 and 11, 1869, respectively.

2. Although Munroe was never permitted to testify in his own defence, he made a statement before the police magistrate on the evening of September 22, 1869, which was witnessed and later recounted by authorities.

3. Abram Craft, statement to police magistrate, October 11, 1869.

4. It is impossible to know how forthright Munroe was with his friends. Of the men assembled, only Craft would later be called to testify, and his account did not include the specifics of this particular exchange.

5. Abram Craft, statement to police magistrate, October 11, 1869.

6. Francis Jones, inquest testimony, October 2, 1869.

7. *Daily Morning News*, September 22, 1869.

8. Ibid.

9. Ibid.

10. In addition to the day's coverage in the *Daily Morning News*, the *Telegraph* also expounded on the respective appearances of the accused.

11. *Daily Morning News*, September 22, 1869.

12. Ibid.

13. The *Daily Morning News* printed Munroe Sr.'s efforts. *Daily Morning News*, September 23, 1869.

14. Robert Worden, inquest testimony, September 22, 1869.

15. Mary Lordly, inquest testimony, September 22, 1869.

16. Ibid.

17. Sarah Collins, inquest testimony, September 22, 1869.

18. Cynthia Dykeman, inquest testimony, September 22, 1869.

19. Sarah Lake, inquest testimony, September 22, 1869.

20. Ibid.

21. Jane McLaren, testimony, September 22, 1869. In some court documents, the surname is spelled "McLarren."

22. Ibid. A sacque is a woman's short jacket that fastened at the neck.

23. Ibid.

24. Hearsay admitted during M.H. Peters's inquest testimony, September 22, 1869.

25. William Lake, inquest testimony, September 22, 1869.

26. James Olive, inquest testimony, September 22, 1869.

THIRTEEN **THE DIE IS CAST**

1. Sylvester Earle, trial testimony, December 14, 1869.

2. *Daily Morning News*, September 23, 1869.

3. Louisa Ells entry, *Lovell's Directory*, 1871; *Daily Morning News*, December 10, 1869; *St. John Daily Telegraph and Morning Journal*, September 25, 1869; *Religious Intelligencer*, June 5, 1857.

4. Louisa Ells, inquest testimony, September 23, 1869.

5. Ibid.

6. Jacob Vail, inquest testimony, September 23, 1869.
7. *Daily Morning News*, September 24, 1869.
8. Jane Campbell, inquest testimony, September 23, 1869.
9. Daniel Hatfield, inquest testimony, September 23, 1869; emphasis added.
10. *Daily Morning News*, September 24, 1869.

FOURTEEN "RUMOURS BOTH GRAVE AND RIDICULOUS"

1. *Daily Morning News*, September 22, 1869.
2. *Daily Morning News*, September 27, 1869. The *Head Quarters* was a Fredericton newspaper.
3. Ibid.
4. *Daily Morning News*, October 2, 1869.
5. *Reporter*, October 4, 1869.
6. Ibid.
7. *Daily Morning News*, September 28, 1869.
8. *St. John Daily Telegraph and Morning Journal*, September 22, 1869.
9. *Daily Morning News*, September 28, 1869.
10. Munroe's supervision of the renovations was recounted during the trial testimony of Thomas McAvity and Sheriff James A. Harding, December 15, 1869.

FIFTEEN A SKULL WRAPPED IN MEAT

1. Coincidentally, the Smith & Wesson was identical to the one Munroe allegedly used, although Christie had no way of knowing it at the time.
2. James Christie, trial testimony, December 11, 1869.
3. James Christie, inquest testimony, September 28, 1869.
4. Ibid.
5. Ibid.; see also LeBaron Botsford, inquest testimony, September 28, 1869. Christie and Botsford should not have tried to estimate calibre from bone. We now know that living bone is far more plastic than it appears in its dry and rigid state when cleaned (or "dead"). Recent studies reveal that entrance wounds in bone can be smaller than the bullet that created them, leading observers to underestimate the calibre of the bullet. See Vincent J.M. Di

Maio, *Gunshot Wounds: Practical Aspects of Firearms, Ballistics, and Forensic Techniques*, 2nd ed. (Boca Raton: CRC Press), 118-19.

6. It is not uncommon for individuals to tamper with, or even shoot, skeletal remains lying in the woods. See R.W. Mann and D.W. Owsley, "Human Osteology: Key to the Sequence of Events in Postmortem Shooting," *Journal of Forensic Sciences* 37 (1992): 1386-92.

7. James Christie, inquest testimony, September 28, 1869.

8. James Christie, trial testimony, December 11, 1869.

9. John March, trial testimony, December 10, 1869.

10. David G. Smith, trial testimony, December 10, 1869.

11. John March and David G. Smith, trial testimony, December 10, 1869.

12. John March, trial testimony, December 10, 1869.

13. Ibid.

14. David Smith, trial testimony, December 10, 1869.

15. Ibid. Recent scientific experimentation proves that Smith was incorrect in his assumptions. Decomposition occurs year-round and in cold climate regions.

16. David Carroll, trial testimony, December 15, 1869.

17. Ibid.; Adam Young, trial testimony December 15, 1869.

18. David Carroll, trial testimony, December 15, 1869.

19. Adam Young, trial testimony, December 15, 1869.

20. *Lovell's Directory*, 1871.

21. Adam Young, trial testimony, December 15, 1869.

22. David Carroll, trial testimony, December 15, 1869.

23. *Daily Morning News*, September 28, 1869.

24. *Daily Morning News*, September 30, 1869.

25. Phileanor Crear, inquest testimony, September 30, 1869.

26. Ibid.

27. Ibid.

28. The clerk's note appears in the handwritten transcript, Queen v. Munro [*sic*], Library and Archives Canada [LAC], RG 13, volume 1408, file 23 A.

29. Phileanor Crear, inquest testimony, September 30, 1869.

30. Ibid.

31. Accusations of coercion and larceny were made during the coroner's inquest testimony of Louisa Ells on September 23, 1869; Philly Crear on September 30, 1869; and Jacob Vail on September 23, 1869.

32. Phileanor Crear, inquest testimony, September 30, 1869.

33. Ibid.

34. *Daily Morning News*, September 30, 1869.

SIXTEEN **PHOTO FINISH**

1. The letter was entered into evidence during Captain H.W. Chisholm's inquest testimony, October 2, 1869. Biographical details of Chisholm's service also come from his testimony.

2. John S. Hall, inquest testimony, October 2, 1869.

3. The unruly morning crowd was well documented in every newspaper, as well as in Day's compendium, 25.

4. *Daily Morning News*, October 2, 1869.

5. H.W. Chisholm, inquest testimony, October 2, 1869.

6. The witnesses were Robert Worden; Mary Lordly; Mary Black, an employee of the Union Hotel; Sarah Lake; and Rebecca Ann Olive.

7. Phileanor Crear, inquest testimony, October 2, 1869.

8. Ibid. Jacob Vail, the sibling, should not be confused with Jacob Vail, the uncle.

9. Ibid.

10. Francis Jones's obituary, *St. John Daily Telegraph and Morning Journal*, February 5, 1885.

11. Francis Jones, inquest testimony, October 2, 1869.

12. A total of fifty-two separate statements were admitted into evidence. In addition, some people (such as Philly Clear) were recalled on more than one occasion.

13. Day's compendium, 30. For whatever reason, Earle's instructions to the jury were not documented in the official transcript.

14. Crown v. Munro, LAC, RG 13, volume 1408, file 23A, 1870.

15. Day's compendium, 30.

16. *New Dominion and True Humorist*, October 9, 1869.

SEVENTEEN **MORBIDITY AND MORTALITY**

1. Each step of the process addressed a specific need. The coroner determined the cause and manner of the victim's death. In homicide cases, the police magistrate determined whether there was sufficient evidence to hold the accused person, pending indictment. The grand jury assessed whether there was sufficient evidence to indict the accused, and the trial was the final determination of guilt or innocence. The grand jury was a panel of sworn jurors (normally twenty-three men) who reviewed the available evidence. The proceeding was closed to the public (and press), and only the prosecution addressed the jury — no defence presence was permitted. The grand jury system has since been abolished everywhere in Canada except Nova Scotia. John A. Yogis, ed., *Barron's Canadian Law Dictionary*, 5th ed. (Hauppauge, NY: Barron's 2003), 151.

2. Humphrey T. Gilbert's obituary, *Saint John Globe*, February 8, 1882.

3. Day's compendium, 30.

4. Sylvester Earle, statement to police magistrate, October 6, 1869.

5. Phileanor Crear, statement to police magistrate, October 7, 1869.

6. *Daily Morning News*, October 8, 1869.

7. *Daily Morning News*, October 12, 1869.

8. Day's compendium, 32.

9. Ibid.

EIGHTEEN **THE OBVIOUS CHILD**

1. See, for example, Munroe's statement of February 14, 1870, in which he wrote, "I do not know that it was actually dead" — "it" being Ella. Day's compendium, 130.

2. For a thoughtful discussion on Victorian-era women, children, and the law, see John Wroath, *Until They Are Seven: The Origins of Women's Legal Rights* (Hampshire: Waterside Press, 1998).

3. Today, most jurisdictions recognize the clinical finding of homicidal violence. It can be the certified cause of death in cases where there are indications of homicide (the actions of another person, such as the burning, dismemberment, burial, or covering of the remains), but no specific morphological cause of death. Were Ella Munroe's body found today in identical circumstances, her death certificate would almost certainly list the cause of death as "homicidal violence."

NINETEEN WITHOUT PEER, WITHOUT QUESTION

1. Jeremiah Travis, *A Law Treatise on the Constitutional Powers of Parliament, and of the Local Legislatures, under the British North America Act, 1864* (Saint John: self-published, 1884); original emphasis.

2. See Sir John Campbell Allen's entry in the *Dictionary of Canadian Biography*, accessed March 20, 2013, www.biographi.ca/en/bio/allen_john_campbell_12E.html.

3. Allen's official portrait hangs among those of his fellow chief justices at the provincial Supreme Court and can be viewed online, www.gnb.ca/Cour/02ChiefJustice/chiefjustices-e.asp.

4. Day's compendium, 33.

5. Ibid.

6. Ibid.

7. Court transcript, December 7, 1869. Jordan's demeanour is also described in Day's compendium, 33.

8. Day's compendium, 33.

9. Court transcript, December 7, 1869.

10. Day's compendium, 33.

11. Court transcript, December 7, 1869, and reprinted in Day's compendium, 33.

12. Court transcript, December 7, 1869.

13. Ibid. Munroe's written affidavit is not in surviving court records.

14. Ibid.

15. Ibid.

16. The occupations and residences of all potential jurors are drawn from local directories and their court testimony.

17. Court transcript, December 7, 1869.

18. Day's compendium, 34.

19. The eleven were: George Quinn, William Peters, Henry Bond, Asa Blakeslee, George Robinson, David Magee, Magnus Sabiston, Peter Chisholm, John Chaloner, John Doherty, and Edwin Frost.

20. Thomas Hannington, James Mulligan, Cyprian E. Godard, and John Manson were excused on grounds of illness. Day's compendium, 35.

21. Court transcript, December 7, 1869.

22. As per Judge Allen's instructions to the jury on December 17, 1869.

23. Thomson had jumped the gun. According to court records, Burpee failed to appear in court when called and was therefore ineligible for jury duty.

24. Isaac Burpee, trial testimony, December 15, 1869; original emphasis.

25. Henry J. Morgan, ed., *The Canadian Legal Directory: Guide to the Bench and Bar of the Dominion of Canada* (Toronto: Hunter, Rose, 1878), 199-200.

TWENTY VICTORIAN GROTESQUE

1. W.H. Tuck, trial transcript, December 7, 1869.

2. See Ben Wilson, *The Making of Victorian Values: Decency and Dissent in Britain, 1789-1837* (New York: Penguin, 2007); Walter E. Houghton, *The Victorian Frame of Mind, 1830-1870* (New Haven, CT: Yale University Press, 1963).

3. W.H. Tuck, trial transcript, December 7, 1869.

4. Albion Neal, trial testimony, December 8, 1869.

5. Ibid.

6. Ibid.

7. Warren Fletcher, trial testimony, December 8, 1869.

8. Day's compendium, 72.

9. Thomas Dallon, trial testimony, December 11, 1869.

10. Bridget Connolly, trial testimony, December 14, 1869.

11. Day's compendium, 86.

12. Bridget Connolly, trial testimony, December 14, 1869.

13. Day's compendium, 86.

14. Bridget Connolly, trial testimony, December 14, 1869.

TWENTY-ONE QUESTIONS WITHOUT ANSWERS

1. Jane McLaren, trial testimony, December 9, 1869.

2. Ibid.

3. Cynthia Dykeman's biographical details from the *St. John Daily Telegraph and Morning Journal*, August 7, 1878, and *Hutchinson's Directory*, 1865 and 1868.

4. Cynthia Dykeman, trial testimony, December 9, 1869.

5. Ibid. A hostile witness shows strong bias toward either party in a trial. Once a witness is declared hostile, counsel is given greater latitude to ask leading questions, and the witness is only required to answer with a "yes" or "no."

Bryan A. Garner, ed., *Black's Law Dictionary*, second pocket edition (St. Paul, MN: West Group, 2001), 771.

6. Cynthia Dykeman, trial testimony, December 9, 1869.

7. Details of George Harding's life and career taken from the *New Brunswick Courier*, July 31, 1830.

8. George Harding, trial testimony on December 13, 1869.

9. Ibid.

10. Ibid.

11. LeBaron Botsford, trial testimony, December 11, 1869.

12. James Christie, trial testimony, December 11, 1869.

13. LeBaron Botsford, trial testimony, December 11, 1869.

14. James Christie, trial testimony, December 11, 1869.

15. Ibid.

16. Modern testing refutes Christie's opinion regarding the rate of decomposition. Field tests and case studies conducted in Canada reveal that a two-hundred-pound individual can be stripped clean of all flesh (largely through the actions of insects and scavenging animals) in as little as one week, even in the depths of winter. See, for example, D. Komar, "Decay Rates in a Cold Climate Region: A Review of Cases Involving Advanced Decomposition from the Medical Examiner's Office in Edmonton, Alberta," *Journal of Forensic Sciences* 43, no. 1 (1998): 57-61.

17. John Marshall, trial testimony, December 11, 1869, which was also the source of the biographical details.

18. Ibid.

19. Ibid.

20. Ibid.

21. Ibid.

22. Day's compendium, 74.

23. John Marshall, trial testimony, December 11, 1869.

24. Ibid.

TWENTY-TWO EVIDENCE OF CHARACTER, CHARACTER AS EVIDENCE

1. John J. Munroe, trial testimony, December 14, 1869.

2. Thomson's closing remarks, December 16, 1869.

3. John J. Munroe, trial testimony, December 14, 1869.

4. Ibid.

5. Thomson's closing remarks, December 16, 1869.

6. Ibid.

7. Day's compendium incorrectly lists Mrs. Munroe's name as Mary Ellen Munroe. Other sources, including her death certificate, indicate her middle name was Eleanor.

8. Both the *Daily Morning News* and the *Telegraph* dissected Mrs. Munroe's appearance and testimony in their coverage December 16, 1869.

9. Mary Munroe, trial testimony, December 15, 1869.

10. Day's compendium, 99.

11. Mary Munroe, trial testimony, December 15, 1869.

12. William Howard, trial testimony, December 15, 1869.

13. Ibid.

14. Day's compendium, 103.

15. On December 16, 1869, both the *Daily Morning News* and the *Telegraph* painted a very colourful (though not terribly flattering) portrait of George Hicks.

16. George Hicks, trial testimony, December 15, 1869.

17. Ibid.

18. Ibid.

19. Ibid.

20. Ibid.

21. Ibid. Kilpatrick worked for John Munroe Sr., although his precise job title was not recorded.

22. Ibid.

23. Ibid.

TWENTY-THREE **"A MAN STEEPED TO THE LIPS IN CRIME"**

1. Day's compendium, 103.

2. John Miles, trial testimony, December 16, 1869.

3. Trial transcript, December 16, 1869.

4. Edward Price, trial testimony, December 16, 1869.

5. Ibid.

6. Ibid.

7. Samuel Thomson, closing arguments, December 16, 1869.

8. Ibid.

9. Ibid.

10. Ibid.

11. Day's compendium, 112. There is a gap in the court transcript at the beginning of Wetmore's closing remarks. Day's reporter also "did not hear some of the opening remarks of the Attorney General" and drew from the *Telegraph*'s report, 110.

12. Day's compendium, 111.

13. Prosecution's closing remarks, December 16, 1869.

14. Ibid.

15. Ibid.

16. Day's compendium, 118.

17. Judge's summary, December 17, 1869.

18. Day's compendium, 126.

19. Ibid.

20. *Daily Morning News*, December 17, 1869.

21. Trial transcript, December 17, 1869.

22. *Daily Morning News* report reprinted in Day's compendium, 127.

TWENTY-FOUR THE VOICE OF REASON, THE VOICE OF THE PEOPLE

1. Entry for Edward Willis by Robert H. Babcock, *Dictionary of Canadian Biography*, accessed June 13, 2013, www.biographi.ca/en/bio/willis_edward_12E.html.

2. *Daily Gleaner* (Fredericton), March 5, 1891.

3. Babcock, "Edward Willis," *Dictionary of Canadian Biography.*

4. Willis's editorial appeared in the *Daily Morning News* on December 20, 1869.

5. Ibid.

6. Ibid.

7. Ibid.

8. Ibid.

9. Ibid.

10. Day's compendium, 127.

11. *Daily Morning News*, December 21, 1869.

12. Transcript of sentencing hearing, December 21, 1869.

13. Ibid.

14. Commentary on Sir John Young can be found in his biography posted on the official webpage of the Office of the Governor General of Canada, www.gg.ca. This is also the source of some biographical information.

15. Ibid.

16. John M. Ward, "Young, Sir John [Baron Lisgar]," *Australian Dictionary of Biography* (Canberra: Australian National University, 1967); *Illustrated Sydney News*, April 16, 1867.

17. Quoted in John Campbell and W. Stewart MacNutt, eds. *Days of Lorne: Impressions of a Governor-General* (Ottawa: Brunswick Press, 1955), 201.

18. A copy of a cover letter from John J. Munroe to the Governor General and the first page of the petition are retained at Library and Archives Canada, RG 13, volume 1408. The specifics of the plea, as well as a description of Munroe's meeting with Young, were widely reported in the press. See, for example, *Daily Morning News*, February 15, 1870.

19. A copy of the petition resides in the national archives. Given the speed with which Munroe secured the names, it is fair to wonder whether all the signatures were genuine.

20. *Daily Morning News*, December 20, 1869.

21. *Daily Morning News*, February 15, 1870, reiterating similar statements the editors had made in the past.

22. Those materials now reside in the LAC Department of Justice master file of the case, RG 13, volume 1408.

TWENTY-FIVE **GIVEN ENOUGH ROPE**

1. *Daily Morning News*, February 15, 1870.

2. Ibid.

3. Ibid.

4. Little, "The Sad Tale of Maggie Vail."

5. *Daily Morning News*, February 15, 1870.

6. Charles D. Grant, "The Cleasby Property," accessed February 19, 2016, www.rothesaylivingmuseum.com/cleasby.html.

7. Little, "The Sad Tale of Maggie Vail."

8. *Saint John Globe*, February 15, 1870.

9. *Daily Morning News*, February 15, 1870.

10. *Saint John Globe*, February 15, 1870.

11. Ibid.

12. *St. John Daily Telegraph and Morning Journal*, February 17, 1870.

13. *Saint John Globe*, February 15, 1870.

14. Day's compendium, 129.

15. Ibid.

16. Little, "The Sad Tale of Maggie Vail."

17. *Daily Morning News*, February 15, 1870.

18. Day's compendium, 129, original emphasis.

19. Little, "The Sad Tale of Maggie Vail."

20. *Saint John Globe*, February 15, 1870.

21. *Daily Morning News*, February 15, 1870.

22. *Daily Morning News*, February 15, 1870; *Saint John Globe*, February 15, 1870.

23. Little, "The Sad Tale of Maggie Vail."

24. *Daily Morning News*, February 15, 1870.

25. Grant, "The Cleasby Property."

26. *Saint John Globe*, February 15, 1870.

27. Day's compendium, 129.

28. From George Munroe's death announcement, *St. John Daily Telegraph and Morning Journal*, March 16, 1895, and his obituary, also in the *Telegraph*, March 18, 1895. See also the death certificate for George Munroe, PANB, vol. 6, no. 378, MF20742.

29. John J. Munroe's burial permit, May 19, 1895, PANB, 1895, vol. 6, no. 526, F20742.

30. *St. John Daily Telegraph and Morning Journal*, May 20, 1895.

TWENTY-SIX *MALUM IN SE*

1. Munroe's confession was reprinted in its entirety in Day's compendium and the *Daily Morning News*. A version of the confession in the LAC master file appears to be a copy. Day's compendium, 129-30; *Daily Morning News*, February 15, 1870.

2. Day's compendium, 129-30; *Daily Morning News*, February 15, 1870.

3. Day's compendium, 129-30; *Daily Morning News*, February 15, 1870.

4. *Saint John Globe*, February 15, 1870.

5. Munroe's confession, reprinted in Day's compendium, 130.

6. From the definition of *malum in se*. Garner, *Black's Law Dictionary*, 435.

7. Arthur Conan Doyle's immortal character was first introduced in 1887, when he appears in "A Study in Scarlet," published in *Beeton's Christmas Annual*.

8. Garner, *Black's Law Dictionary*, 360. Canadian law says the same thing in a different way: "The Crown is only required to prove the necessary mental element (*mens rea*) of the offence, which is distinct from motive." Yogis, *Canadian Law Dictionary*, 183.

9. The theory does not ignore or override the fundamental requirement that the accused be deemed "sane" under the law. "Insanity," in this context, is a legal rather than medical standard. To be legally sane is to have the mental capacity to understand the nature and effect of one's actions, typically assessed by the defendant's ability to distinguish right from wrong.

ILLUSTRATION CREDITS

FIG. 1 (page 18) Detail of plate 3, modified from F.B. Roe and N. George Colby's *Atlas of Saint John City and County, New Brunswick, 1875* (St. John, NB: Roe & Colby, 1875)

FIG. 2 (page 20) Photograph of John A. Munroe, 1860s. Provincial Archives of New Brunswick, image P571-1.

FIG. 3 (page 57) Photograph of a re-enactment of the discovery of the bodies on Black River Road, 1869. Provincial Archives of New Brunswick, image P571-3.

FIG. 4 (page 65) Photograph, described as "skull found at the murder scene of Sarah Margaret Vail," 1869. Provincial Archives of New Brunswick, image P571-2.

INDEX

photo: Dan Froese

DEBRA KOMAR is the author of *The Ballad of Jacob Peck*, *The Lynching of Peter Wheeler*, and, most recently, *The Bastard of Fort Stikine*, which won the 2016 Canadian Authors Award for Canadian History. A Fellow of the American Academy of Forensic Sciences and a practicing forensic anthropologist for over twenty years, she investigated human-rights violations for the United Nations and Physicians for Human Rights. She has testified as an expert witness at The Hague and throughout North America and is the author of many scholarly articles and a textbook, *Forensic Anthropology: Contemporary Theory and Practice.*